DICTATORS

AND

DEMOCRACIES

TODAY

The Author

DICTATORS AND DEMOCRACIES TODAY

By

JOHN MARTIN, B. Sc.

Lecturer and Consultant on International
Relations at Rollins College

Essay Index Reprint Series

BOOKS FOR LIBRARIES PRESS
FREEPORT, NEW YORK

First Published 1935
Reprinted 1968

D
443
.M362

TO MY WIFE

*without whose persistent assurance I should not have
believed that audiences would assemble to hear
unsensational lectures, nor students
be found to read them.*

LIBRARY OF CONGRESS CATALOG CARD NUMBER:

68-16953

PRINTED IN THE UNITED STATES OF AMERICA

INTRODUCTION

By

RAY STANNARD BAKER

THE genesis of this book is interesting and significant. Five years ago, in the winter of 1930, Mr. John Martin, Professor of International Relations at Rollins College, Florida, held a series of conferences on the relationship of the United States to varied and serious problems of foreign affairs. They were intended only for students. In following years adults, by request, were admitted; lectures were added; and this spring (1935) it was impossible to seat all those attending any one of the ten lectures in the largest auditorium in Winter Park. The audiences included college presidents and professors, writers of national reputation, lawyers and ministers, financiers and eminent women. Cars brought regular listeners from resorts thirty to fifty miles away. This book consists of the material, somewhat enlarged and revised, used by Mr. Martin in his addresses.

It is doubtful, if one combed the country over, whether there could anywhere be found a more impartial, or realistic, or better-tempered treatment of the highly controversial affairs of this troubled world than Mr. Martin gives us in this volume. Some of those who attended the lectures may have taken issue with certain of the speaker's interpretations; no one doubted the objectivity of his approach or the sanity of his outlook. A treatment without a trace of propaganda, its sole purpose was to broaden understanding and clarify thought.

To some of those who listened to the lectures, as I did, the profound interest invoked was scarcely secondary in its significance to the subject matter presented. American consciousness of foreign affairs, and interest in them, is of recent growth. Prior to 1914 the nation was abysmally ignorant of the world outside its boundaries and suffered grievously as a result of it. Since then, and especially in the last three years, there has been a rapidly growing awareness that we live in a newly crowded world wherein we may be easily injured by the jostling of restless neighbors. A new anxiety, a new resolution to understand, represented by these extraordinary audiences at Winter Park, has been developing, and in itself is one of the truly hopeful evidences that Americans are determined to master their problems and solve them, as in the past, by orderly democratic methods.

These lectures and the book growing out of them seem perfectly designed to secure that "creation and rule of the best opinion," which Woodrow Wilson considered the chief objective of free discussion in a democracy. Without such a foundation of measured understanding the nation can scarcely be prevented from slipping, one way or another, into the slough of dictatorship. It would be fortunate, indeed, if this book could be placed in the hands of leaders of opinion throughout the country.

WINTER PARK, FLORIDA
APRIL, 1935

CONTENTS

Chapter   Page

FRONTISPIECE: *The Author* iv

INTRODUCTION BY RAY STANNARD BAKER . . . ix

BIOGRAPHICAL SKETCH xiii

Part I—The Machinery of Peace

I   The League of Nations and the Kellogg Pact in
Perspective 5

II   The Breakdown in Disarmament . . . 25

III   Must the United States Fight Japan? . . 27

IV   Wanted: A New Strategy of Peace . . 65

*Part II—Three Dictatorships and Three Democracies—the Foundations
of their Domestic and Foreign Policies*

V   Russia and Communism 89

VI   Italy and Fascism 111

VII   Germany and National Socialism . . . 131

VIII   The Democracy of France: Liberty, Equality,
Fraternity 153

IX   Democracy in Great Britain: Law, Order,
Parliament 173

X   Democracy in the United States: Life, Liberty,
the Pursuit of Happiness . . . 193

XI   Youth and Dictatorships: A Challenge to
Patriotism and the Leadership of Youth in
America 215

INDEX 223

BIOGRAPHICAL

JOHN MARTIN *was born and educated in England, where he taught first in the public schools and, later, in the East London Technical College. He was active in the London Fabian (Socialist) Society, sitting on its executive committee with George Bernard Shaw, Sidney Webb (now Lord Passfield), Sidney Olivier (now Lord Olivier) and James Ramsay MacDonald, now Prime Minister of England. Mr. Martin was chairman of the Labor Party in Hackney, a municipal division of London, and a member of the Borough Council.*

In 1899 he came to the United States, upon invitation, to lecture at various colleges and clubs. In 1900 he assumed direction of the League for Political Education in New York City; and married Prestonia Mann, of New York. He became a citizen of the United States in the shortest legal time.

Writing and lecturing and committee work in connection with numerous social welfare societies, accompanied by membership of the Board of Education of Greater New York, gave him experience in the American way of conducting public affairs. In collaboration with his wife he wrote a book on "Feminism". When the Great War ravaged the world its toll of wounds, misery and death made these labors for better social conditions seem to him petty and puerile. What use to save the lives of a few babies with pure milk campaigns and mothers' aid if a war could torture and slaughter more babies in a week than all the welfare societies could save in a decade? Why worry to train boys in better schools if they were, ultimately, to be sacrificed in a bloody holocaust?

For five years Mr. Martin withdrew from all public activities and kept silent while he studied the new world situation. International matters, which, before the war, were hardly noticed by ardent idealists, came to seem to him equally important with domestic affairs. So, at Rollins College, he concentrated his mind and thought on the problems of peace and war, and the dealings between nations. This book is one of the annual harvests.

PART I

THE MACHINERY OF PEACE

CHAPTER I

The

League of Nations

and the

Kellogg Pact

in

Perspective

Dictators and Democracies Today

CHAPTER I

The League of Nations and the Kellogg Pact in Perspective

WHILE the Christmas chimes, ringing out the message of Peace, still echo in our minds, it is timely to recall that today, January 10, is the fifteenth birthday of the League of Nations, a body that was organized, as the preamble to its covenant states, "to promote international cooperation and to achieve peace and security." Note, not to guarantee peace, but to *achieve* peace, a word which indicates work continued over a period for the attainment of a distant object.

Ever since the conception of such a league originated there have been two conflicting ideas as to the best means of achieving peace. At the first meeting of the League to Enforce Peace, held in Philadelphia while the World War was still raging, that division arose; and the president of the American Peace Association with some of his friends left the room, saying: "You cannot achieve peace by making war. You cannot *enforce* peace upon the nations of the world." But the League of Nations was established in conformity with the idea that peace might possibly be enforced. Woodrow Wilson accepted the conception; England and France accepted it; and the covenant was drafted with that principle embodied.

It is often overlooked that the Covenant provides amply also for arbitration, conciliation, judicial determination of disputes, and envisages the use of force only as an ultimate. But still that use is contemplated. Article 16 says:

"Should any Member of the League resort to war in disregard of its covenants . . . . it shall *ipso facto* be deemed to have committed an act of war against all other Members of the League, which hereby undertake immediately to subject it to the severance of all trade or financial relations, the prohibition of all intercourse between their nationals and the nationals of the covenant-breaking State, and the prevention of all financial or personal intercourse between the nationals of the covenant-breaking State and the nationals of any other State, whether a Member of the League or not."

The nation resorting to war in breach of these covenants is to be sent to Coventry, boycotted in the family of nations. Further, if that fails, "It shall be the duty of the Council to recommend to the several governments concerned what effective military, naval, or air force the members of the League shall severally contribute to the armed forces to be used to protect the covenants of the League."

Thus, in addition to the peaceful methods, forcible methods of compelling adhesion to the covenants were contemplated.

This provision was obnoxious to a number of sincere supporters of peace efforts who predicted that it would not work. It is a mistake to suppose that they were in any sense opposed to the maintenance of peace or to effort for such maintenance. They merely differed as to the method by which peace could be achieved. By 1928 they had evolved a method of their own, called The Outlawry of War. When Senator Borah had been won to the conception of the Outlawry of War, favorable circumstances brought it to the attention of M. Briand, foreign minister of France, and, after negotiations too long to be detailed, the nations of the world were brought, practically all of them, under the lead of the United States, to renounce war as an instrument of national policy, to make war no longer legal under international law. The high contracting parties agreed that they would seek the settlement of their disputes or conflicts, no matter what their nature or what their origin might be, exclusively by pacific means. And thus the principle was embodied in the treaties that the force of world opinion would be sufficient to persuade the nations to refrain from war, to settle all their conflicts and disagreements entirely by pacific means.

Before examining the history of the last 15 years and its expression of the effectiveness or ineffectiveness of these two principles, let us look at the main pacific means which was immediately established, even before the Kellogg Pact, by the League of Nations. So soon as the League was organized it set to work to establish a World Court, a Court of International Justice. It succeeded because, especially through the splendid work of our elder statesman Elihu Root, the method of selecting the judges of the court was agreed upon. Five judges with four deputies sit permanently at the Hague. These judges are available all the time to hear causes presented by the nations of the world. Previously there had been no such court. States in disagreement about the interpretation of a treaty had no judicial body to which they could immediately and directly appeal. But now that judicial body has been set up. It has worked successfully since January, 1922, when it held its first session. It has determined cases of great importance and complexity. A year ago it determined, as between Denmark and Norway, the ownership of the east coast of Greenland. It awarded that coast to Denmark. Norwegian patriots were, many of them, seriously aggrieved that Denmark should be allotted that icebound coast. But the premier of Norway instantly accepted the judgment and further dispute upon it was avoided. On another occasion France and Britain were in conflict as to citizenship in Tunis, the matter which is now disturbing Italy and France. France claimed that any person born in Tunis of two parents, one of whom had also been a French citizen, would automatically become French. That conflicted with the rule of Great Britain which considered that the loss of British citizenship was always a disaster and must be avoided to the extreme. France claimed it was a domestic question, and it was therefore submitted to the court to determine whether this question of citizenship was domestic or international. The court ruled, perhaps adroitly, but in accordance with treaty and law, that the question was domestic; but that the domestic action of France must be determined and motivated according to any treaty

7

on the subject which France had entered into, and that France had already entered into a treaty which embodied the British view on the subject. Both states accepted the decision and the thing was settled.

In addition to determining cases the World Court is authorized to give advisory opinions to the Council or the Assembly of the League. An advisory opinion is just such as a person or corporation would go to its lawyer to procure when it was in doubt about the legality or illegality of some course of action it proposed. So the League, or Assembly, or the members through the League, can ask the court as to the legality or illegality of certain contemplated actions in order that its constitution may make their action strictly legal, strictly in accord with the international law which the court interprets.

Probably the most delicate advisory opinion given yet—and more advisory opinions have been given than decisions—was rendered between Austria and Germany. When Austria and Germany announced their determination to combine economically, the objection that at once was raised was that this was contrary to treaties into which Austria had entered, especially one treaty which had been made by Austria in consideration of a large international loan which had been raised for her benefit. Great Britain suggested that the matter be placed before the World Court for an advisory opinion. Most Americans, I think, at the time felt that Austria was being hardly treated, that if Austria wanted to make an agreement with Germany to enter her economic system it was harsh to prevent Austria from doing it. But the court, by a decision of eight to seven, decided that the various treaties which Austria had made barred this action by Austria.

It was argued at the time by some that this decision was rendered according to national interest. Mr. John W. Davis has made an analysis of the decision which proves beyond cavil that no case at all could be made in support of the claim that the national interest of the judges had prevailed. Belgium and France were on opposite sides, which surely would

8

not have been the case, since they were in close alliance, had national interest prevailed. China and Japan were on the same side, that is to say, the judges of Chinese and Japanese nationality were on the same side, which would hardly have been the case had they been looking to any national interests. It was a close case, but was decided judicially. Today I think that those who regarded it from its political aspects have probably changed their views and are glad that Austria was not absorbed by Germany two or three years ago. However, the advisory opinion was given purely on legal grounds.

In January, 1926, the United States Senate voted for American adherence to the World Court, making five conditions. Four of these conditions, which were minor, were promptly accepted by the other nations. The fifth was to the effect that no advisory opinion should be rendered in which the United States had or claimed an interest, without previous consent of the United States. After prolonged negotiations, in which Mr. Elihu Root again played a noble part, a method was arranged by which the United States would be amply protected, and yet advisory opinions might be rendered when other nations desired them. The American Bar Association and other associations have declared that this formula is perfectly ample, but the United States Senate Foreign Relations Committee has held the matter in committee during four or five years.

Notice that the World Court does not involve the conflicting views as to the reliance upon moral force or the use of physical force in the attainment of peace. It has no police or army at its service. It necessarily depends upon the good faith of the litigants for the acceptance of any decision. And in the long course of arbitrations and of judicial decisions on international quarrels, I believe there has not been a single case in which the litigants have rejected the decision when rendered.

What has been the history of the effectiveness of the Covenant and the Pact? Twelve months ago both were at their lowest ebb in prestige, for, be it recalled, whatever failure the Covenant has shown, that failure has been fully shared by the Pact.

A year ago Germany and Japan had withdrawn, or given notice of withdrawal from the League, the Disarmament Conference was at apparently an unbreakable deadlock, the Chaco war was dragging its slow bloody length through the years, and many people were disposed to say, "The League is dead. Its uselessness has been demonstrated." Now let us see briefly what were those events which discredited the League and the Pact alike.

In 1928, when the Chaco War broke out, the Secretary General of the League sent word to the combatants calling their attention to their obligations under the Covenant, and for a time the embers died down. At the same time the Pan American conference was in session, and the League deferred to that conference and to the United States as a leader in that conference, for action upon the matter. Action was taken, vigorous and continuous, but without avail. In 1932 the war broke out with fresh fury and is raging still. All through the years the Pan American delegates, the neutrals of America, the United States, and the World League have cooperated, but events have shown that even the embargo on arms to the combatants, an embargo in which the United States joined lately, has not been applied with sufficient force and in sufficient width actually to stop or even, apparently, to curtail the fighting.

Japan in 1931 made war upon China. Immediately all the powers of persuasion which the League of Nations could evoke were used. Japan defied the world. Japan defied public world opinion as well as any potential threat of force. For seventeen months the League of Nations exerted itself. Japan was brought to the bar of the League and of the world not once but several times. Japan claimed she was acting in self-defence, thereby taking refuge in the reservations which many nations made concerning the renunciation of war in the League and Pact. She claimed that she was not making war. War was never officially declared.

Thereupon Sir John Simon suggested an amendment to the Covenant to provide against the use of force, rather than the use of war; but since the Kellogg Pact already provided against the use of force of any kind, it seems vain to think that would have made any difference.

Mr. Henry S. Stimson, Secretary of State, throughout that Japanese controversy cooperated heartily with the League. He even provided the leadership which Great Britain rather hesitantly followed, but which Great Britain finally followed in company with its fellow League members. His doctrine of non-recognition of territory acquired in contravention of covenants is still maintained; and Manchukuo, the puppet state, is not recognized in its independence and integrity by the other nations of the world.

But force was used; war was actually waged, whether it be called war or not. The League Covenant proved ineffectual; the Kellogg Pact proved ineffectual. And so we were driven to take a new view of the situation. Even the boycott, the severance of all commercial and financial relations, could not be agreed upon. England in particular strenuously objected to such a breach of its relations with Japan. So we were driven back to consider anew: "What is the most available and ultimately, perhaps, the most effectual means of achieving world peace?"

Within the last six months in particular the prestige of the League has risen fast on account of several consecutive events: First, the success of the League itself in resolving the difficulties in the Saar region and the dangers arising out of the assassination of Alexander the First of Jugoslavia; second, the accession to the League of one of the greatest powers in the world, Soviet Russia; third, equally important, the increasing hearty cooperation of the United States in the League's activities.

Let us review them briefly:

The Saar is a region about two-thirds the size of Rhode Island but with a population of 830,000, making it one of the most densely populated parts of Europe. It includes rich coal ores and is strategically, lying as it does between Alsace Lorraine and Germany, of great importance to both of these countries. When the peace treaty was under consideration France demanded that the Saar basin be ceded to her. Lloyd George and Wilson objected, but ultimately a compromise was effected. France argued that the French coal mines had been devastated, that they would take ten years to get into proper order again, that the malice of Germany in destroying those mines should not be overlooked; and, therefore, it was agreed that the Saar area should for fifteen years be ceded to a League of Nations commission for rulership, and that in 1935 the people of the Saar should vote whether they wished to return to the jurisdiction of Germany, to remain under the League of Nations, or to become French.

As the time for the plebiscite approached there was considerable tension in the Saar, and for some weeks it appeared as if war would be almost inevitable before its fate could be settled. All through the summer of 1934, after the accession of Hitler to power in Germany, the German Front in the Saar was very aggressive and impudent. Terroristic acts were committed; blatant oppression was exercised, and Geoffrey G. Knox, the English official who is chairman of the Saar Commission, complained frequently that, unless an armed force of some sort aided him, he could not maintain order until Sunday, January 13, 1935, when the vote was taken. The story runs that last summer (1934) an eminent member of the British government went to a German Spa and there met Mr. Knox, who was also taking the cure. It then dawned upon this English minister that the Saar was an outpost of British rule which was being left without his government's protection and support. So, within a few days after the return of the minister, Scotland Yard sent a bodyguard to see that no Hitlerite should, in a moment of passion, attempt to assassinate Mr. Knox and so throw Europe into disaster.

Later, the French and the Germans—Laval representing France—got together and decided politically the disputes which were most acute concerning the Saar. It was agreed

that the mines should be paid for by Germany with 900,-
000,000 gold francs when the Saar is restored. It so happens
that these coal mines have been state mines ever since 1750,
and so it will be very easy to transfer ownership from the
government of France to the government of Germany. It
was agreed by Hitler that there should be no molestation of
any inhabitant of the Saar, for a year at any rate, on account
of race, religion, or nationality.

When that was settled Great Britain had a change of
heart. To the astonishment of the whole world Great Britain
reversed the refusal to send troops to aid in the maintenance
of order, and agreed that 3300 troops should be sent, the
largest batch from England, a somewhat smaller batch from
Italy, and batches from other countries to make up the 3300.

That international army was on the spot, a week or two
before the election. Disorder and riots broke out, national
feeling ran high; but a peaceable vote was cast. The vote was
in favor of restoring the jurisdiction of Germany. That jurisdiction was restored peacefully and the question of sovereignty was settled without any resort to arms.

At the same session of the Council of the League the Jugoslavian dispute was determined. On October 9 Alexander I
of Jugoslavia landed at Marseilles to pay an official visit to
France. He was accompanied by Louis Barthou, French foreign minister, who had been most active for some weeks in
making agreements with various countries of Eastern Europe.

Through almost incredible negligence, the carriage was
not guarded adequately along the quays of Marseilles, and
a terrorist, rushing from the sidelines with a shout of "God
save the king" to camouflage his intentions, shot both the
king and the foreign minister to death. He was immediately
set upon by the infuriated crowd and his life extinguished.
A passport was found in his pocket which revealed that he
was a Croatian terrorist. Inquiry subsequently showed that
he had been trained in a camp for terrorists within the territory of Hungary, just across the Jugoslavian line. The Jugoslavian nation was united in sorrow and indignation against

this nefarious deed. Previously there were marked divisions between the different nationalities which make up the composite Jugoslavia, but the blood of the king cemented the people. At once bitter indignation was expressed against Hungary. Jugoslavia retorted by sending, somewhat brutally and callously, across its border some 2000 Hungarians who had been working in Jugoslavia. Threats were made to send back 20,000, since Hungary was claiming that the presence of Hungarian citizens on Jugoslavian soil warranted return of that soil to Hungary.

Fortunately the Council of the League was sitting. Appeal was made by both countries to the Council; long negotiations followed. Threats were hurled. Benes, the notable foreign minister of Czechoslovakia, said bluntly that he who changes the mileposts along the frontier evokes war. Hungary could not be permitted to use any means, terroristic or otherwise, for the change of the boundaries as settled by the Treaty of Versailles. Finally, at midnight on December 10, 1934, a conclusion was reached. It was decided by a resolution formally adopted by the whole League membership that the gallant Alexander I, the unifier, had been assassinated without cause, without justification; that some Hungarian officials, through negligence, had made themselves partly responsible; that Hungary could be trusted to visit punishment upon such neglect; that no nation had the right to harbor in its midst any groups dedicated to terrorism for political ends; and that a commission should be established to draft a law which the nations might adopt on this subject.

For forty-eight hours any gun that went off on these fevered frontiers might have brought on war. But war was avoided, and the League thereby demonstrated that, if it be not able to prevent all wars, it can prevent and has prevented some wars.

Russia has strengthened the League immeasurably. Russia seeks peace, for the present at any rate, that it may pursue its domestic policies without hindrance. Japan on the East and Germany on the West threaten Russia, and Russia decided that for its own better protection it must seek the fold of the family of nations within the Covenant. Thus the defection of Germany was partly compensated for.

But of greater interest to us is the increased prestige of the League due to the ever-increasing cooperation of the United States. In May, 1934, by joint resolution of Senate and Congress, the United States became a member of the International Labor Office. This office was established when the League first came into being, largely upon the insistence, certainly with the active aid of Samuel Gompers, who was the President of the American Federation of Labor. The idea is that fair competition between nations in commerce is inconsistent with gross differences in wages and other conditions of labor in the divers countries. Further, that the discontent which arises where social injustice is heavy breeds civil war and international war, and peace must be established upon a basis of social justice. That sounds very much like the doctrine of the New Deal, and there is little wonder that the American Administration did last May put us into the International Labor Office.

The convention which controls the office is made up of four delegates from each government, two from each group of organized employers, and two from each group of organized workmen in the different countries. The purpose is to recommend statutes to be adopted in the separate countries concerning such things as night labor for women and children and hours of labor—eight a day or forty a week, etc.—and conditions of health in factories.

Much of this work has been done. The office is housed in a magnificent building in Geneva. The present secretary is Mr. Harold Butler, who is an Englishman and succeeded the French Socialist, M. Thomas.

The United States is in the International Labor Office— went in without any blare of trumpets or beating of drums.

The United States has been one of the most active and effectual members of the Disarmament Conference of the League of Nations. Mr. Norman H. Davis, our delegate, has been most active, and has made fruitful suggestions. Finally President Roosevelt authorized him, in the name of the United States, to present a complete treaty for adoption under which the manufacture and sale, especially the export, of all munitions of war would be subject to national license within each country, and subject also to international supervision by a commission, which commission would operate under the Secretariat of the League of Nations, and to the expenses of which commission the United States would contribute its share.

It is too late to discuss the isolation of the United States. No such isolation longer endures. We are in the League of Nations in everything except formal membership, always, however, subject to a reservation which Norman H. Davis has reiterated more than once in this past summer. The United States is concerned exclusively with the promotion of peace, and not with the waging of war even in the name of peace. The United States is taking no part in the political or domestic affairs of another nation. The United States took no part in the Saar controversy, nor in the Jugoslavian decision. The League without the United States was entirely successful. I suggest to you that we who have sought peace through the decades should adjust our minds to the new historic situation of the United States. The United States is today one of the most powerful agencies in the world acting deliberately and continuously for the promotion of peace. Our object is not the glorification of the League of Nations. Our object is to achieve peace and security. To that object formal membership of the League is not a pre-requisite. As a matter of fact, let it be noted that the League's greatest successes have been won where the United States was not involved. And the League's failures have come, as it happened, where the United States was working in cooperation most heartily.

It is delusive to say that if the United States were only a member of the League, all difficulties would vanish. The United States was in effect a member of the League during the whole of the Japanese embroglio, and that was the most conspicuous failure in the League's history. It is too derogatory of the other nations of the world and too flattering of the United States to pretend that the United States' formally filed membership is essential to the avoidance of war, and would ensure the avoidance of war. It is hardly accurate to argue, as some have done, that unless the United States should join the League, war within fifteen years will be inevitable and unavoidable; but if the United States should join the League, then such disaster would be averted. Let us recognize that, despite the neglect by the United States during the early Harding Administration, the League has grown in vigor and power; and that the World Court has functioned admirably during a decade, although the United States has passed by on the other side.

The League is now growingly recognized to be an agency for the promotion of international cooperation, in which respect it has succeeded almost entirely as regards the United States. International cooperation through the League by the United States has grown month by month. Both the hopes of the friends and the expectations of the enemies of the League have been belied. The League has not succeeded in preventing all wars. The League has not succeeded in developing any practical means by which an offending nation could be unitedly boycotted or by force of arms brought to its knees. But the League has prevented a number of small wars that might have become big wars.

The League is the only representative body which ever approximated a Parliament of Man, the only agency through which the smaller powers, some of them as strong morally as they are feeble physically, can influence world opinion and world decision. When France appealed to the League in April, 1935, after Germany had repudiated the Treaty of Versailles, the unanimous condemnation of Germany by the Council expressing the moral reprobation of mankind, following the earlier precedent of the condemnation of Japan's action in Manchuria, strengthened the rule of reason against the rule of force; though it may not, alone, be effective to curb Hitler. Only by broadening from precedent to precedent may the League acquire power.

The League must work slowly, developing experience. We have found that we cannot jump into the millenium. A large number of Americans, in the national habit, hoped and expected that we had in the League a mechanism which would guarantee perpetual peace, just as many ardent total abstainers hoped and expected that in Prohibition there was a mechanism which would guarantee national abstinence. Human nature cannot be changed or brought under discipline with that rapidity. The League is invaluable in the world. The association of the United States with it is of the highest value. But, if we look at the matter historically, are we not bound to recognize that by trial and error, by the pragmatic method, we in the United States have discovered how to cooperate in the maintenance of peace without incurring the dangers which many of our foremost citizens foresee in complete absorption into the League? I take it that Woodrow Wilson was too patriotic to desire that the United States, contrary to Washington's immortal advice, should involve itself in the political affairs of Europe. The United States has been slowly working out a way by which, while keeping entirely free from those political affairs, we do cooperate with them in every agency which directly tends to the achievement of peace. It is essential that the mind of the American people be carried along as these methods are slowly, even rapidly developed.

We are proceeding in conformity with our divided view, securing united action by acting cautiously. The League itself has recognized through its members that the use of force is impracticable. In the last year numerous new pacts are being negotiated. France is negotiating today a pact of mutual assistance in the East. These pacts indicate that the nations themselves in the League are doubtful of the efficacy of the League Covenant, and that they have proceeded to strengthen themselves by additional covenants.

But this is no cause for despair or deep-seated disappointment. Just as in place of Prohibition is being substituted the slow work for individual temperance and detailed methods of suppressing drunkenness, so we are recognizing the peace of the world can be achieved only by laborious continuous effort. However, we console ourselves with the conviction that, ultimately, after decades of consecrated labor, the millenial condition may be attained of which we sometimes sing:

"*For lo! the day is hastening on*
By prophet bards foretold
When, with the ever-circling years
Comes round the age of gold,
When peace shall over all the earth
Its ancient splendor fling
And the whole world give back the song
That now the angels sing."

CHAPTER II

The

Breakdown

in

Disarmament

CHAPTER II

The Breakdown in Disarmament

In the last year (1934) two disarmament conferences have been in session, one at Geneva, the other at London. At Geneva the subjects of discussion have been land, water, and air armaments, with a special emphasis upon land arms and armaments. At London the topic has been exclusively naval armaments. We will consider them in order.

When, three years ago, the Geneva conference assembled, millenial hopes were entertained that at last the world was in sight of a reduction in the implements of death. American women signed petitions by the hundreds of thousands, naively expecting that their influence would be as potent in international halls as in the halls of the American Congress. But, alas, after three years of dispute and discussion and effort—honest effort on the part of many statesmen—no conclusions have been reached; no treaty has been signed.

Various proposals were made in the course of the negotiations, embodying different principles for determining the issue. The effort was made to distinguish between offensive and defensive weapons. This occupied some months, and was finally abandoned. It was found impossible to determine whether a six-inch gun was defensive, and a gun with an eight-inch mouth for vomiting fire was offensive; whether a 25-ton tanker was objectionable to humanity, and a 20-ton tanker relatively harmless; whether an airplane of only fifteen tons weight, stripped, was no serious menace, whereas a heavier plane was the agent of the devil; and so through the gamut of weapons. It was finally a cause for scoffing at Geneva when anybody mentioned a distinction between offensive and defensive weapons.

Then it was sought to limit the national budgets and

25

thereby effect reduction of armaments and arms. This effort was frustrated, even if it ever had any chance of success, by the depreciation of various national currencies, which evidently made it impossible to measure accurately how much additional or less was being expended each year by those nations on armaments. An elastic yardstick is clearly incapable of measuring accurately.

Through it all the United States was cooperative, assumed leadership, and accepted responsibilities. Its record has been honorable and praiseworthy. In the first year President Hoover proposed that the arms of the world be reduced upon the basis of establishing first, what force was necessary for the maintenance of domestic order, and second, what additional force was required for exclusively defensive operations. That Hoover proposal was the rallying point of the nations who sought the more radical, more effective, more drastic methods of disarmament. When a less general and more academic statement had been drawn up as the conclusion of the first six months of the conference, Litvinov, the Russian delegate, and those who supported him put forward the Hoover proposal as the alternative, which, however, under the rule of practical unanimity, could not be passed.

The second year, 1933, was the year of the British scheme. Mr. James Ramsay MacDonald, irritated with the failure to agree on anything specific, brought forward a voluminous treaty which included practically every factor of the problem, from the fundamental of security to the last gadget on the last rifle.

With respect to security it had always been argued by France and her satellite nations that if only the United States would agree to confer when troubles arose, with a view to union with the other nations in the repression of an aggressor, that then real advance could be made. So President Roosevelt authorized our able and active delegate, Mr. Norman H. Davis, to say that, on condition that specific disarmament were actually accepted, the United States would be committed by presidential proclamation to conference with the other powers whenever the Pact of Paris or the Kellogg Pact were violated; and, further, that the United States would agree that, in the event of the League of Nations instituting blockade or armed chastisement of an aggressor, if the United States also agreed that such a nation was the aggressor, then the United States would forego the neutral rights on which it has hitherto in all wars insisted and would in no way interfere with the action of the League of Nations in bringing the aggressor to terms. That was for the United States a remarkable, a farsighted, and, in view of the feeling of members of the U. S. Senate, a daring concession.

The British program was debated for months. Fundamentally the problem was: What shall be the size of the different continental armies? Upon that problem the utmost diversity of opinion was expressed. In every case and on all the subjects it appeared, on analysis, that each nation was perfectly willing to have the kind of force reduced which was specially valuable to some other nation, but was always reluctant to reduce the kind of forces which, in its own circumstances, were potent. It would be too tedious to attempt the review in detail, but one major issue we may refer to. By the Treaty of Versailles the standing army of Germany was reduced to 100,000 men. This was to be an army of long-time enlistment—twelve years. You may remember that after the Napoleonic Wars the reverse policy was pursued against Germany—Germany was forbidden to enlist an army for a longer period than three years training for each man, and the Prussian leaders thereby established what has become the standard continental system of calling up the whole manhood of the nation for three years' training, keeping them in reserve as they grew older. So Lloyd George said: "Let's take warning from that history and insist that Germany now shall have exclusively 100,000 men of twelve years' training and service." France objected but was overruled, and the Reichwehr became an army of 100,000 enlisted for twelve years. Experience, however, has led the French to view that army with greater alarm than they would a conscript army. War has become more scientific; its instruments more complicated. Training counts increasingly, and so the French insisted at the disarmament conference that the Germans should accept a relinquishment of that long-time enlistment and should return to the short-time conscript method.

Then there arose the problem: "Which men should be counted in the armies?" The French said, "Those men who have served their time and have returned to civil life, although they may be called up as reserves upon the outbreak of war, should not be counted among the armed forces. Similarly, our black troops in Algeria and Tunis and Senegal should not be counted among our forces because they are across the Mediterranean on another continent, although we did bring them across the water to fight with us in the Great War." "On the other hand," said the French, "Germany has Storm Troops with black jackets and helmets who are regularly practised in army maneuvers. All Germany is practising the goose step, and so all Germany may be counted as one armed camp." With such conflict of opinion, what wonder no agreement was reached!

So 1933 passed and the nations seemed to be no nearer the goal. 1934 was the year of the awakening of the nations to the menace of armaments manufacturers and traders to the whole cause of disarmament. The Senate investigation of the United States stirred the world. Officially, for the first time, to the whole of the peoples was revealed the irreconcilable conflict between the interests of munitions makers and the interests of peace makers. Hitherto it had been the practise of governments and of peoples to assume that the making and trading, importing and exporting of the deadliest powders, the hugest battleships, the most lethal bombs was on a par with the making and trading of food, clothing, and agricultural machinery. And the governments acted on that assumption. The munitions makers themselves did not dream that when they were arming a potential enemy, they were acting unpatriotically. Mr. Dupont, who personally is no doubt an honorable man and a patriot, ready to sacrifice himself, his sons, his business interests to the defense of the United States, showed amusement and anger and chagrin when it was hinted in the Senate inquiry that the action of his companies in exporting powders and T. N. T. and the rest was inimical to the interests and the defense of the United States.

But the revelations showed that this red traffic in death did degrade and demoralize the minds of some of those engaged in it. They made secret arrangements to thwart and evade the embargo on arms to Bolivia and Paraguay which the United States Government approved in May, 1934. They had arrangements with foreign makers for the exchange of secret processes, and occasionally they won business by revealing even the secrets of the War Department. They established in good business fashion, as far as they could, monopolies. They arranged to pay subsidies to each other, to share profits if competitive bids for submarines for Spain were not entered. They acted for the promotion of their own personal and company financial interests. They are not in business for their health; neither are they in business for the promotion of American or English or French defense. There is a conflict of interest which is absolutely irreconcilable, as irreconcilable as slavery and freedom.

In 1934 the nations began to consider how this traffic could be brought under control and made subordinate to the national interest. President Roosevelt in 1934 again took the lead. He presented to the Disarmament Conference the complete text of a treaty, which he proposed should be adopted, which provided that in a munitions-making country the manufacture should be subjected to national license; that all imports and exports of arms and munitions should be reported to the government and made public; that, in order to insure that every nation should aid by its agreement, an international commission, permanent and authoritative, should be appointed; that this commissoin should have the power of making an inspection periodically in every country which had signed the treaty; that it should make special inspections when any country complained to it that the treaty was being violated; that this commission should operate along with the permanent officials, the Secretariat of the League of Nations; and that its expenses should be paid by a special levy to which the United States would gladly contribute its share.

We peace-seekers may glory in the record of our government in this matter of disarmament. There has been a standing offer, first made by Coolidge, renewed by Hoover, accepted by Roosevelt, that this country will submit to any limitation of its navy to which the other nations will likewise agree. I remember that I was in England when Coolidge first made that offer, and, when I mentioned it, even informed peace-workers expressed their astonishment. They said, "When was the offer made? We have not heard about it." I could point to the official communication, of which the British press had taken scant notice.

What was the fundamental reason, apart from all the staggering, bewildering details, for the breakdown at Geneva? It was the political differences, particularly between France and Germany. Germany had declared it would be satisfied with nothing less than equality of armament, recognized by the other powers as its right and need. France had insisted that the first essential was French security, combined with the security of other nations. Even when Bruening and von Schleicher were the chancellors of Germany they had raised this issue of equality. Von Schleicher, who on June 30, 1934, was assassinated on a trumped-up charge of treason, was among the first to assert Germany's irreducible prerogative. When Hitler came to power he reasserted with more vigor that same claim, and never could the French and the German demands be reconciled. France said and has always said: "The order must be, arbitration, security, disarmament. First security, then disarmament." So in October, 1933, Germany finally disrupted the conference by withdrawing from it and giving notice of resignation from the League of Nations. Thereafter the whole problem was, "Is it possible to make a disarmament treaty in the absence of Germany, and could Germany be brought back into the League."

The conflict between those views remains. Fundamentally the Allied states of the war are in antagonism to the defeated states. Italy at one time showed a tendency to support Hungary in a demand for a realignment of frontiers, but the bloody events in Austria changed Italy's mind. Italy could not brook a union of Austria with Germany, which would bring the German frontier down to the Italian Tyrol.

A new alignment was reached within the next months which, paradoxically enough, promised to procure the return of Germany to the Conference and a final agreement on the disarmament question. It seemed to be a victory for both sides. Later England and France and Italy agreed that they would make a pronouncement to the effect that the military restrictions of the Versailles Treaty, after thirteen to fifteen years of peace, should no longer be imposed on a defeated nation; that they would support the claim for open rearmament of Germany on condition that Germany should return to the League of Nations, present its case to the League, and accept the decisions of the League upon the subject. France has always insisted that the Treaty of Versailles could not be modified by one-sided action, that only the League itself is competent to modify that treaty. England endorsed that view.

Germany might have said: "We don't care how it's done so long as it be accomplished." Hitherto France had resisted the recognition of any right to rearmament by Germany. At this point in the negotiations, however, France considered two factors: first, Germany was rearming and it would be foolish to shut one's eyes to the fact; second, the position of France in Europe was greatly strengthened. A league of foes had been formed around Germany. Hitler, unconsciously, had been the greatest peace agent in Europe and was entitled to the Nobel Peace Prize, for his actions had brought Italy, France, and Great Britain into an agreement, had brought Russia into the League, and had brought Hungary to the consciousness that changes of boundaries attempted by force would bring a united Europe, practically, against the aggressor.

So there was, temporarily, a more cheerful outlook. From the storm clouds had come flashes of lightning which had revealed new aspects in the landscape. At the moment, the outlook was brighter than when the disarmament conference assembled three years earlier.

Suddenly, however, Germany again repudiated the method of agreement and charged the European air with fear of war. On March 16th Chancellor Hitler announced that Germany would proceed immediately to create an army by conscription which would be half a million strong and equipped perfectly with all modern weapons. He would not wait a week to obtain the sanction of the other powers under the terms of the Treaty of Versailles. He threw off all pretence of abiding by the Treaty and issued a Declaration of Defiance. For forty-eight hours all Europe talked of war. But Great Britain kept cool. The cabinet met on Sunday—sacrificing the precious week-end in the country, as is never done except in great emergency—and resolved to wait and see.

It had been already arranged that Sir John Simon, the Foreign Secretary, should visit Berlin and try to bring Hitler to accept the offer already made for bringing back Germany into full partnership in the family of nations. The immediate question to be determined was whether, Hitler having taken the bit between his teeth, the visit should still be made. It is authoritatively reported that Prime Minister MacDonald and Mr. Stanley Baldwin, President of the Council, advised that the visit be cancelled; but Sir John Simon was keen to carry out his plan. So, Chancellor Hitler's cold, (caused, it was rumored, by the issue of England's somewhat tactless White Paper) being better, the engagement was confirmed.

France and Russia were perturbed by Britain's amiable reception of the Hitler coup. They were mollified by an agreement that Sir John Simon should call on Hitler in company with Sir Anthony Eden, the Lord Privy Seal, that Sir Anthony should proceed to Moscow and Warsaw, for exploratory conversations, and that at Stresa, on Lake Maggiore, on the eleventh of April, France and Italy should receive a report on the outcome of all the conversations.

The interview at Berlin revealed, to a startled England, that already the German airfleet, illegally built, was equal in strength to the British airfleet, and that the foreign policies of Germany and England "were in disagreement." Hitler insisted that Communism is the enemy of civilization and that western nations should cooperate with Germany in resisting and overthrowing this common Russian foe. As to German rearmament he was frank to brutality. He made it plain that Germany intends in future to raise, train and permanently sustain a force, military and perhaps naval, as powerful as the Kaiser's before the war.

The German people have received Hitler's program with rapturous acclaim. Ever since the armistice they have felt humiliated and downtrodden. That their great nation and their proud army should be beaten to the earth was to them, always, an injustice, a mystery, an unnatural calamity that almost shattered their faith in the Most High. Never have their leaders accepted the defeat. Generals and Junkers have proclaimed that only the treachery of Jews and Social Democrats could explain the disaster. Surely the mighty, noble, sacrificing army and its supermen on the Great Headquarters General Staff were blameless. Only traitors behind the front accounted for the collapse. Hitler was the loud megaphone for this legend. His rise was the answer to the German peoples' yearning for reassurance of their broken spirit; their nostalgia for the old, blundering, sabre-rattling Prussian officers' arrogance. They longed to assert themselves once more as a power great by virtue of its military might. And Hitler has answered their yearning. Again the goose-step resounds on every road.

Europe's reply is to ring Germany round with armies too strong to be defied. England, no longer secured by the silver channel; England, with its frontier moved back from the white cliffs of Dover to the rushing waters of the Rhine, was compelled, though reluctantly, to move side by side with France. Hitler's airplane menace is as alarming as the Kaiser's naval menace. So the agreement to pool air fleets, that France and Italy and England offered to Germany on condition that Germany should settle other differences in friendly fashion, may be made effective without Germany's partnership. And the Eastern Locarno, the plan to sustain the existing boundary lines in Eastern and Central Europe, except as they may be changed by mutual consent, while open always to Germany's accession, may go into effect as between the countries involved, except Poland and Germany—with Britain's sanction, but without Britain's signature.

Even Poland is hinting that Germany's one-sided restoration of conscription and armed power is not conducive to good relations. While Russia, thoroughly alarmed, and convinced that Germany, in collusion with Poland, may at any time make a raid on the Ukraine, shows keen anxiety to induce Britain to throw its weight against the old foe.

So Europe is back to the discredited ancient ways of its diplomacy, the method of alliances and of the balance of power. Security and peace by cooperation seem for the time to be hopeless and discredited. However, immediate war is unlikely. Had France been willing to start a preventive war the time to have acted was in May, 1933, when General Weygand, its highest military leader, recommended such a war. Germany needs several years to launch and train its new army. Russia wants quiet for the development of its internal plans. No nation sees a stake worth the awful appeal to arms. War scares will blaze up and die down like fires of straw; but actual fighting will probably be postponed indefinitely.

Most dangerous will be the situation when Hitler repudiates the Locarno agreement, to which Germany was a willing, free party in 1925. Under that agreement a strip of territory east of the Rhine fifty miles wide and the whole of Germany next to France west of the Rhine is to be kept free from military preparations. No armed men or forts or guns are to wound its rustic calm. Should either Germany or France pollute this buffer area with soldiers both Italy and England are under pledge to resist the treaty-breaker with arms.

Will Hitler observe this pledge? Or will he in new defiance raise troops, build barracks, mount artillery, construct fortifications, alleging that as France has a line of impregnable forts a few miles behind its frontier, Germany is entitled to a line equally strong a few miles within its frontier?

Should he act in conformity with his recent practice he will go ahead in secret while protesting his love of peace and will expect to face the nations with a *fait accompli*. But France and England through their secret intelligence departments will know what he is doing and France will demand that England honor its signature. That will put England "on the spot."

Britain is pestered with chains of newspapers, yellow and bellicose, which advocate the renunciation of the League and the Locarno engagements. These papers vociferously demand, daily, a policy of aloofness from continental affairs. But the preponderant public opinion, as shown recently by a wide and dependable poll, supports membership of the League almost unanimously, and, with slightly less unanimity, economic sanctions against a war-maker.

Technically, the militarization of the peace zone would not be war; as Japan's attack on Manchuria was, technically, not war. But, obviously, it would be a breach of a treaty voluntarily signed for Germany by Chancellor Streseman, which cannot be repudiated on the claim that it represents only the victor's chains riveted upon the vanquished. The League Covenant does not bind the nations to boycott or to fight a treaty-breaker. Yet the League Council in April, 1935, appointed a committee to explore the practical expedients in enforcing an economic and financial boycott against Germany, in the event that Hitler shall make anticipated further defiance; because the Council judges that a militarized Rhineland would presage war.

Efforts to lure Germany back into cooperative paths of peace may be expected to fail unless Hitler is convinced that Britain will act in unison with France, Italy, Russia and the Little Entente. Already Germany is hard pressed by the failure of its foreign trade; and is perilously close to an inescapable inflation and the breakdown of its internal economy. Should London rupture financial and trade connections, along with other nations, almost surely German industry would collapse. If the lords of the Ruhr are convinced that Britain would concur in a boycott they would, in all likelihood, hold Hitler back from a further aggression which would ensure their own ruin.

Should extreme measures be adopted America also will be driven to be either for or against Germany. If the rest of the western world boycotts Germany will American citizens jump in to capture all its financing and business? That will be a new problem. Hitherto Britain has stoutly refused to use its navy for the service of the League unless assured in advance of the attitude of the United States. May Britain make the same condition with respect to a boycott of Germany? That would be a brand new aspect of the old problem of neutrality.

Recent nation-wide discussion of neutrality shows that the American public is awaking to its importance, that the public is learning that tranquil relations with other nations do not hang upon a preference for tranquillity, however intense, but rather upon pursuing national policies that will foster tranquillity. America cannot trade with nations at war, and make them loans at high interest rates except at the risk of itself getting into their war. Quite possibly that quandary will have to be faced also with respect to an international trade and financial boycott. Shall America support commercially a nation which the League has decided must be held at arm's length, outside the family of nations, until it revokes the measures that will provoke war? It is fortunate that the current discussion is preparing the public mind. Slowly the difference between the interests of a few, eager to profit from world disaster, and the interests of the whole American people is being discerned. If implanted in the public mind, the conception that the profits of a small minority of manufacturers and traders do not constitute a national interest—if, indeed, not actually against the national interest—may change American policy, both in peace and in war.

Meanwhile, is it possible that some larger formula will be evolved by which all the nations may be brought into agreement to go their ways without war? Can England quiet the snarling kennel? Will the longing of all the plain people for peace prevail over the warrior readiness for conflict? Even the German folk dread another slaughter. Even Hitler would avoid battle if only he can win his goal by bluff and diplomacy. Fortunately the staff of the strengthened Reichswehr has a realistic view of military problems. It is unlikely to permit Germany to put the issue to the sword when the odds are heavy against victory. So long as France, Italy and Russia, with England in the background, are united against any German aggression, Hitler will be held in leash; and, in the period of waiting, the influences for peaceable adjustment of differences should work strenuously without respite.

What a dismal distance is this situation from the radiant dreams in which the League of Nations was born. How discouraging! But also how challenging! America's contribution will surely be to stand beside the nations, whichever they be, that will accept reason and treaties, persuasion and agreement, for their weapons. Possibly the American government, officially, can give little advice or aid. Europe must reduce its hates and angers and suspicions and fears before the disarmament conference, in which alone the American administration can act, will again function with promise. But the opinion of America, expressed through church and forum and press, will be a welcome support to the harassed peace forces across the Atlantic. Their plight is desperate. They merit our sympathy.

To return to the disarmament conferences of 1934.

In London the naval conference between Great Britain and the United States and Japan was held. In 1922 and 1930 treaties of armament reduction were negotiated respecting navies. The official outcome was this: In great battleships of 35,000 tons, the mammoths of the deep, equipped with every gadget that science can devise, carrying great guns which will shoot accurately for twenty miles and more, Great Britain and the United States agreed to have an equal tonnage; Japan agreed to have 60% as many tons in these capital ships. The same percentage was accepted for airplane carriers, the huge floating platforms which carry airplanes as hawks were carried on the wrist in the Middle Ages, that they may reach within striking distance of their quarry and then, shooting into the air, may drop death on their victims. Big cruisers form the next category, ships of 10,000 tons and over, carrying 8-inch guns, cruisers that can steam long distances without refueling. Upon these the United States lays special emphasis, because it lacks the naval bases over the world which the English nation can utilize. Of these big cruisers the ratio was to be 10-10-7, 70% being accepted as Japan's allotment. The same ratio of 70% was accepted by Japan for destroyers, those wasps of the ocean that shoot at enormous speed backward and forward to defend the mammoths against torpedo and submarine attack, the destroyers which insured the safety of the American troops as they were ferried across the Atlantic in 1917 and 1918. Finally, submarines were declared to be primarily defensive weapons, and all three powers agreed to construct only equal weights of those undersea destroyers.

In each nation the navalists made strong objection to the treaty, but that objection was most vocal and powerful in Japan. There a cabinet was overthrown on the issue and only after months of hesitation was the treaty signed, and then mainly in consequence of the limited approval given to it by old Admiral Togo, who is to Japan and the Japanese navy what Lord Nelson was to Great Britain and her navy. Togo died in May, 1934, at a very old age, nearly ninety, loaded down with honors and the veneration of the Japanese people. They entered into a national celebration at his state funeral, which has not been equaled in the history of Japan. He had procured the acceptance of these limited navies for the period of the treaty only. And so, when the renewal of the treaty came up, Japan was already determined. In May of the previous year she had startled the assembled diplomats at Geneva by stating that the treaties of Washington and London should not be called up for reconsideration. Japan considered them outside the agenda of Geneva and, in any case, not suitable to the newer conditions, and Japan announced that it would ask a larger apportionment in any new treaty. So inquiries were made in 1934 in anticipation of the formal conference to be held in 1935. Japan has denounced the treaties, or, in other words, has given notice that she will permit the treaties to expire at the end of their announced term.

Now what is being gained by these treaties? Not an actual reduction in the building of naval vessels: neither England nor America has actually built up to the limit set up by the treaties. We who thought that the treaties fixed a framework within which the navies would be built without criticism and without national ascerbity were mistaken. I doubt personally whether on the actual building in Great Britain and the United States the treaties have had any influence except, (and the exception is important), that no nation has built or will lay down a 35,000-ton post-Jutland mammoth capital ship. But the treaties had this most important influence: they stopped a possible rivalry in building between England and the United States. They mollified the growing antagonism over the claimed predominance of the American fleet. America had asserted that she was going to build a fleet second to none on the seven seas. Before the World War the United States fleet was the fourth among the fleets of the world. And when we are judging Japan's demand for equality we should remember that Japan is only faithfully following the United States' example. It is only saying to the United States, "Me too." For towards the end of the war the United States, without any change of conditions of importance, out of the blue declared one morning that the United States was going to be satisfied in future with nothing less than absolute equality with the British fleet, and if the British didn't like it, then we would build a fleet stronger than theirs and see whose purse would last the longest. The great advantage of these naval treaties was that that antagonism and competition was allayed. In the second place we must admit that the American fleet has been built for the last decade with a fight against Japan primarily in view. We insisted on the major importance of capital ships; capital ships could be used to fight on the other side of an ocean 3500 miles wide. Which ocean do we propose to cross? The Atlantic, to fight in the confines of the Irish Sea and the English Channel; or the Pacific, to fight in the waters of the China and Japanese Seas? We have insisted that great cruisers of 10,000 tons are our favorite weapon because, as we have frankly announced, they also could be steamed across 3500 miles without refueling. They also may be utilized not for the defense of the American coasts, but for the attack upon Asiatic coasts.

Now if we are to have a war, it were better, doubtless, that the war should be fought many miles from our own coasts. But when we argue with the Japanese that they have equality of security, which is our main contention for the retention of the old ratios, we are bound to confess that we are trying to arrange that we shall be able to reach their shores, and we are not taking into consideration at all their possible ability to reach our shores.

The Japanese, of course, recognize these facts; it is no use for us to blind ourselves to them. We may hardly look for any modification of the Japanese demand for equality of naval armament. The council superior to the elected diet, composed of elder statesmen, princes, and potentates close to the body of the divine emperor considered and determined the problem before the London conversations of 1934 were opened, and we may not anticipate that, in front of us, they will reduce that claim of equality any more than, in front of Great Britain, the United States will reduce its claim of equality. Why? Because Japan has laid out a century-long program of empire development, because she judges that her policies, of which her navy is an instrument, demand that she shall be dominant on the eastern flanks of Asia. Only by the settlement of these political matters can the settlement of the naval matters be procured. Political questions determine. So the United States is faced with a dominant problem of its international relations: Must the United States fight Japan either this year or a decade hence? That question, of overwhelming imporance to us, I shall attempt to answer in a later chapter.

CHAPTER III

Must

the

United States

Fight

Japan?

CHAPTER III

Must the United States Fight Japan?

In 1930, when the naval treaty had been signed at the London Conference, Japanese patriots showed deep resentment over the acceptance by their delegates of what they called a position of inequality and inferiority. Since Japan agreed to be satisfied with a navy sixty per cent as strong as the British and the United States navy, a lieutenant, to advertise his mortification, committed hara-kiri in the corridor of a railroad train. To the chief naval negotiator a dagger was presented as a suggestion that only by himself committing suicide could he redeem his honor. A little later a student invaded the office of this admiral and committed hara-kiri by disemboweling himself in the presence of the admiral's secretary.

This was the beginning of a fever of heated nationalism. The military party gained strength month by month, and the attack on Manchuria supervened. Thereafter dissension which aggravated the naval quarrel arose over the antagonism between the military powers and the industrial powers.

Japan is almost owned by five great houses, chief of whom are the Mitsui and the Mitsubishi. The military in Japan are the leaders of the peasants. They are not, as in most countries, the policemen for the dominant economic interests. They are the spokesmen for the revolting, hungry, oppressed peasantry. When Japan went off the gold standard the house of Mitsui netted some hundred million yen by its financial manipulations. To show the patriotic indignation an assassin took the life of the vice-president of the Mitsui house; others assassinated the executive of the Mitsubishi house, perfectly willing themselves to give their lives if they could but rouse and express the national indignation. A party of forty-seven

47

military cadets and sailors invaded the home of the old prime minister Inukai, seventy-three years of age, and deliberately shot him down as he was murmuring: "Should you not take off your shoes to step on my mats? Surely shooting is not necessary. Then take a cigarette." And he fell dead.

The emotional frenzy came to a climax when these forty-seven were tried in the Autumn of 1933. Petitions said to contain a million signatures were presented to the court for clemency to the offenders. Signatures were written in blood by frenzied women. Fingers were cut off and sent wrapped in silk floss to the court along with the petitions. The offenders were let off with light sentences and will probably receive promotion. In their defense they charged that this ministry which they had so assailed had betrayed the interests of the nation, and that it had been subordinate to the Anglo-Saxons. The universal cry was for a firm front in face of the West; and the United States was represented as Japan's main actual and potential foe.

We Americans ask in amazement, "How can that be?" We are conscious of no hostility to the Japanese people nor, as we judge, any antagonism to their real interests. And yet, if we take a historic backward look, we shall find some ground for Japanese resentment.

Since 1906 America has repeatedly blocked the path that Japan attempted to pursue. Japan was convinced that the interference of President Theodore Roosevelt prevented them from procuring an indemnity from Russia after Russia's defeat. Presently arose the trouble over school textbooks in California and the demand of Californians that Japanese must not be admitted to the same benches as Aryans. When war broke out in 1914 Japan was an ally of England. In the course of the war Japan expelled Germany from Shantung. It presented to China twenty-one demands which, if granted, might have established Japanese suzerainty over China. The first news of these twenty-one demands was a scoop for the newspaper representative of the Associated Press. The president of the Associated Press took them to William Jennings

Bryan, then Secretary of State, who called the Japanese ambassador and asked: "Is it possible that this is true?" The ambassador asserted the dispatch was false. Later on, being chided by Secretary Bryan for his lies, he made the excuse that he had obeyed instructions.

Before the end of the war Japan proposed to invade eastern Siberia. President Wilson ill-advisedly sent an army of ten thousand Americans to take part in that invasion. The Japanese, thereupon, increased their army tenfold. Friction between the American and Japanese forces developed. At the peace conference America demanded that the Japanese should evacuate Shantung and eastern Siberia and should renounce the twenty-one points. The formal renunciation was not obtained at the peace conference and, on the return of President Wilson, he was roundly abused by the liberal opinion of America for not having insisted peremptorily upon the immediate withdrawal by Japan of all their demands in China. A little later Japan did withdraw from Siberia, partly on account of her inability to fight at forty below zero in Siberia and to repel the aggressive Bolsheviks. But the United States was the chief nation which expressed hot indignation concerning Japan's procedure.

In 1922 the United States pressed Great Britain to terminate its treaty with Japan. British dominions joined in the pressure, and at the Washington conference Great Britain renounced the alliance. Two years later, in 1924, the United States Senate wounded without necessity or advantage the tender pride of Japan by classing Japanese with orientals unfit to be admitted to United States soil, refusing to adopt the expedient of setting a quota for Japan as for other nations and so saving Japan's face.

When Japan invaded Manchuria the United States was the leader of the world's opposition. The United States it was that announced the policy of non-recognition of territory taken in violation of treaties. In all these measures the United States has been convinced of its own integrity and nobility. It has been sure that imperialism practiced by Japan was an offense against international morality. By its Manchurian and Chinese campaigns Japan offended precisely those elements in our population which would naturally, instinctively, be friendly to a foreign power. It alienated the peace seekers of the United States by torpedoing the peace structure which had been slowly and painfully erected. Thus, while Japan has been growing resentful and angry against the power of the United States, the population of the United States has been becoming increasingly distrustful of Japan.

No wonder, then, that European observers talk about the inevitable war between Japan and the United States. Judged by these recurring conflicts of policy it would seem as if the dread arbitrament of force might ultimately be reached. However, no war is inevitable, and this war will not be permitted to occur. When two trains approach from the far ends of a single track, a collision, to an ignorant onlooker, might seem inevitable. But one train pulls aside on a sidetrack and the other passes by in safety. The United States will see that one of these threatening trains shall be sidetracked and the collision be averted.

To do that, however, we must ourselves examine the fundamentals of our policies in the Far East. We have two years' respite before the naval treaties expire. In view of the exasperated sentiments of the Japanese population, we need not anticipate any subservience and not much compromise from Japan. Foreign Minister Hirota, in his speech to the Japanese Diet in January, 1935, carefully pointed out that their purpose was to procure further naval disarmament. They only asked that Great Britain and America abandon ships of all sorts until their own fleets are brought down to a parity with the Japanese fleet, and that such a demand is surely in consonance with the policy of disarmament.

He did not point out that such equity on the part of the three fleets would give undoubted dominance to the Japanese fleet in the Western Pacific Ocean. Nor did he point out that the crucial difference between Japan and the United States is related to Japanese policies on the Asiatic continent, and that the purpose of Japan's demand is to permit Japan to carry through its policies without interference or intervention from western powers. So we are faced in these next two years with the inescapable necessity for examining the bases of our own policy, the reasons for this twenty-five-year-long obstruction and belittling of Japan. In doing that we must take into account several factors.

First, let us get into our consciousness the fact that the Japanese are not inferior little yellow men. The Japanese are a highly intelligent people, a race with characteristics as notable as distinguish any western people. The Japanese have loyalty deep-seated, intelligence highly trained; their literacy is greater than that of any other nation; they have industry and inventiveness, love of order and cleanliness, devotion to family and reverence for law, and a willing subjection to their heaven-sent ruler which distinguishes them among the nations of the world. In eighty years they have leaped from the sixteenth century, a nation full-panoplied, performing a miracle comparable to the leaping of the goddess full-panoplied from the head of Jove.

Japan surely merits respect as a nation equally with western powers. To estimate the quality of its breed look at a splendid specimen. Noguchi, born in poverty, deserted by his father at birth, was left in the care of his young sister. As a toddler he falls into the charcoal brazier on the floor, one hand is burnt off, the other rendered useless, and scars disfigure his body. At the age of twelve he is treated by a medical man who has just received western training. The use of his one hand is restored, and he thereupon renounces the soldier's vocation which is the ambition of every proud Japanese boy, and determines to devote himself to the science which had been utilized to his body's salvation.

He finds occupation in a drugstore as an errand boy. He studies the pharmacopœia. He is sent by steerage passage to America, at the cost of a neighboring peasant who sells his clothes to raise the money. He goes to an army doctor in Philadelphia and says, "Here I am. I want nothing but my food and lodging and the chance to study medicine." He remains there, rather a troublesome problem, several years; for, like other Japanese, is is proud as Lucifer, touchy in the extreme, temperamental as an opera singer. But eventually he is brought to New York, to the Rockefeller Medical Research Institute, and becomes one of the great men of science of the world. He is credited with discovering the yellow fever germ and other germs of importance. He develops the serum for yellow fever. He is told that that serum might not be suitable for West African fevers. He insists that he will go himself and try it, and segregate the germs of the African variety. Before doing so he returns to Japan. He goes back to pay reverence first to his old mother. The old peasant who had aided him refuses to accompany him to the great banquet across the inland sea, and so Noguchi returns and bows to the ground before the peasant in token of reverence and honor. Then he sails for Africa along with an American. They try out their methods, and both of them die, martyrs to science.

The temper of Noguchi is the exaltation of the temper of the Japanese people. Just as Theodore Roosevelt was the American raised to the Nth power, Noguchi was the average Japanese raised to the Nth power.

In determining, then, our treatment of this issue, we may accept the fact that we are dealing with equals, not with men inferior because their skin is of different color. Second, we may make plain, if possible, to the Japanese that we admit to the full their national right to life, liberty, and the pursuit of happiness. We have no wish, indeed, nothing could be farther from our thoughts, than to destroy Japan. We know that the seventy millions cramped in those small islands cannot be fed and sustained by home produce, any more than England can be fed today from its own soil. We may regret, but we admit, that the Japanese population is increasing by one million a year. We know that under those circumstances outlets either for people or industry must be discovered by Japanese statesmen. We are not going to deny the right of Japan, because Japan is a newcomer, to trade around the world. Japan is making a vigorous drive for export outlets. Japan has not particularly inconvenienced the United States, though we did object to electric light Christmas tree bulbs and tennis shoes and bicycles being deposited here at prices ridiculously below anything which our manufacturers could match. Within our own territory we have our own remedy. But we are not going to declare that Japan shall not sell cotton goods to India or the Philippines, to the east and west coasts of Africa, or in the islands of the south seas. Other nations may be terribly inconvenienced by this new competitor who is operating on the principle of freedom of trade, of selling at the lowest price, which was the accepted gospel of the West throughout the nineteenth century; but the United States is not specially molested.

We may possibly consider a revision of our prohibition against any Japanese immigration. There are only 135,000 Japanese in the country today, most of them in the neighborhood of Los Angeles. If we salve Japanese pride by giving them a quota, they would only be entitled to 187 immigrants per annum, and Canada's experience with the same expedient indicates that the number coming might fall far short of the quota. Without approving Japanese sensibilities we can anyway take cognizance of them and utilize them for our purposes in our diplomacy. If a concession in form of that sort will stir their gratitude, is it not good business as well as good diplomacy to make it?

More fundamentally, we may take cognizance of, inquire into and analyze the bases of the policies which have produced the clashes between the United States and Japan.

They may be all summed up in the one word: "China."

The United States, for reasons which are not entirely clear, has taken China under its benevolent protection. When John Hay announced the Open Door Policy we were beginning our spasm of imperialism in imitation of England. We were setting out on a career of stimulated international trade. We thought that European nations had sinister designs on China. Japan was hardly then in the reckoning. We suspected that England, Germany and France would divide up China into spheres of influence, and announced: "That we shall forbid. We will maintain the territorial integrity and the administrative and political independence of China. This shall be one tenet of American foreign policy."

When the twenty-one demands were made, Secretary of State Bryan reiterated that American policy to the Japanese ambassador: "The territorial integrity and political independence of China is the charge of the United States." In 1922, under our leadership, that principle was written into the nine-power treaty. Paradoxically enough, the administration which was shuddering with horror at the thought of taking any part in the League of Nations and guaranteeing the territorial integrity of any European country, committed the United States by treaty to a special care of the territorial integrity of the unmeasured and imperfectly bounded semi-continent called China. The United States has asserted that authority ever since; and today it is part of the traditional policy of the United States State Department, though, fortunately, there are indications that the State Deparment is preparing to abandon that policy.

Our State Department, through the mouth of Mr. Norman H. Davis, told the conference in London in the last months of 1934 that the United States would not assume the sole responsibility for checking the expansionist ambitions of Japan. He laid exclusive emphasis on the commercial side. Attention may be called to the other factor.

Our policy has been supported for reasons of humanity as well as for reasons of trade. Our missionaries have supported the State Department in asserting a protectorate over China's territorial integrity. That policy was successful until Japan invaded Manchuria in 1931, but what has been the result to China? Since 1912 China has been the most chaotic region on earth, barring the fighting zones during the Great War in Europe. China has been devastated: armies, sometimes ragged and primitive, sometimes well set up and armed with modern rifles, have swept crisscross through those 480 millions with rapine, loot, massacre. Every atrocity known to the Middle Ages has been visited upon these helpless swarming peasants and workers. In one city a few years ago in Shantung the women and children were so mistreated by the soldiery that they finally leapt down the wells and choked them with their dead bodies to obtain relief. That kind of thing has been terrorizing the population hither and yon throughout that vast territory. If we realized what has been happening in China our sleep would be frightened with hideous nightmares.

News from China, given in Hirota's Diet address in January, 1935, was that for the moment the war lords had been subdued and only the communist armies remain. These armies are mislabeled and libeled as communists. They are mainly peasants in revolt. These agrarian rebels, defeated in two main provinces, trekked towards the southwest, where they joined other bands in distant Szechuan. It may not be wise to judge between those warring groups in China, those bellicose, feudalistic war lords and their minions, but is it not clear that if American purpose has been humane, sadly has that purpose missed its aim? When we recall what has happened to Shantung, can we be certain that America showed humanity in compelling Japan to withdraw from Shantung? When we realize that Chiang Kai Shek, the commander-in-chief and sometime president of the Nanking Government, refused to fight the Japanese troops at Shanghai, that the valiant Nineteenth Route Army, which made an effective, heroic stand against the invaders, was afterwards destroyed by Chiang Kai Shek himself when it joined the opposing side in the civil war; when we remember that Chiang Kai Shek purchased by popular subscription a number of American airplanes, for the announced purpose of fighting Japan, and that the first use made of these planes was to destroy that Nineteenth Route Army, the one army to which the American heart leaped in sympathy when it stood to defend its soil at Shanghai; when we remember that Chiang Kai Shek is a sworn blood brother of Toyama, the president of the Black Dragon Association, the super-patriotic organization of Japan; when we notice that within a year the Chinese Government has granted to Japan trading privileges which give Japan advantage over all the other nations; then we are brought to wonder whether Uncle Sam may not have been at various times a sentimental fool in his dealings between China and Japan.

Of this we become certain: Never will we sanction a war for the sake of sustaining China.

Now look at the commercial side: American interests in the Far East are relatively negligible. When we took the Philippines and entered upon that short career of active imperialism, we dreamed of unlimited markets in China. We harbored, as one man and one woman almost, that pathetic economic illusion of the nineteenth century that one nation could be enriched by providing cotton shirts for millions of outsiders. We had calculations of the prosperity that must follow if only every Chinaman would buy one more blouse a year. But all these dreams have vanished. We now recognize that our venture in the Philippines was a business loss, and we are prepared to leave the Philippines in ten years. Our total trade with China is only about $105,000,000.00 a year. Allow ten per cent profit on it—$10,000,000.00. It doesn't pay the costs of patrolling the Yangtse and maintaining our ships in Pacific waters, to say nothing of the capital value of the ships and the overhead. British interests are from six to twelve times as great, economically, as American interests, in different parts of East Asia. Britain is resentful and alarmed at that upspringing, sword-waving newcomer, Japan; but the United States can afford to stand aside and let George V do it! Dutch interests far exceed American interests, for their immense rich Asiatic colonies are threatened; while French investments in China are only slightly less than American investments, and French Indo-China, which France has no intention to evacuate, may be menaced by the Japanese navy.

Mr. Norman H. Davis has told the European countries that we will not accept sole or main responsibility for checking Japan navally, but that we will cooperate with the other nations. As Mr. Walter Lippman has pointed out, this change of policy is momentous, one of the most important diversions in the history of our diplomacy. In the next two years,—if we as a people fully comprehend these matters,—we shall be prepared emotionally to reach an amicable, mutually profitable agreement with Japan. We and the rest of the world may have to accept some humiliation; we may have to renounce our policy of non-recognition of Manchuria. Japan is making that easier by insisting that Manchuria is an independent state. When the policy was announced by Secretary of State Stimson President Lowell of Harvard opposed it vigorously, declaring that it was improper, unenforceable, and would ultimately have to be withdrawn. President Lowell may be vindicated by history.

But, in cooperation especially with England, and with France and with Holland also we can probably persuade Japan that her best interests will be served by working in agreement, as far as possible, on naval matters with other countries. In point of fact, Japan today is at greater advantage with respect to Great Britain and America on navies than she would possibly have been, had no treaty been negotiated in 1922. Japan will perhaps recognize, when the elder statesmen are permitted to put their minds on the problem, that the United States could outbuild her over and over again, if driven to do it. Japan's pride cannot withstand the guns of a battleship, and America could, if challenged, outbuild Japan more than five to three.

But the world is trying to adopt a more rational system of settling differences, including some organization and cooperation. Japan is one of the newest comers among nations, and the newest comer among great powers. Japan may be led to accept the new attitude of cooperation. The American people feel nothing but friendship for the people of Japan. We don't want to compel them to starve in their island home. We only ask that their exploitation of China shall be made with consideration for Chinese sensibilities and for the interests of other powers.

Our first duty is to our own country. We are hindered in our efforts at cooperation by the perfidy which Japan has shown more than once. We cannot afford to leave ourselves helpless. Our navy must be maintained in strength, in order that we may talk with Japan in the gate. California will never be exposed to be served as Manchuria was served. Under all the circumstances even peaceseekers must endorse the action of the Roosevelt Administration in proceeding to build up the navy to treaty strength. We asserted in 1922 and 1930 that a navy of a certain strength was requisite for our protection. We agreed with the other nations that that strength was reasonable. We make no objection to other powers building up to their allotted strength. Japan has built up to that strength, practically to the last ton. Therefore there can be no just criticism of the United States in proceeding to build up to that strength and so backing up the word and the judgment and the promise of our negotiators. We are not going to trust blindly to the honor of Japan; for that honor Japan has violated. We can be quite candid about that. Russia has protected eastern Siberia by arming eastern Siberia. Russia by now, according to the best-informed judgment and opinion, would have been invaded by Japan, had not eastern Siberia been well supplied with bombing planes with a radius that would reach Tokio and Kyoto and Nagasaki and might in one night put these cities to the flames. So the United States Government cannot neglect home defense.

America may aim to be noble, proud, dignified, but not obstreperous; determined to defend to the last gasp its home shores if necessary, but not committed to carry warfare thousands of miles across the ocean nor to fight anybody else's wars either in Western Pacific or Eastern Atlantic.

CHAPTER IV

Wanted:

A New Strategy

of

Peace

CHAPTER IV

Wanted: A New Strategy of Peace

PEACE seekers were greatly discouraged by the defeat in the United States Senate of the motion for joining the World Court. By seven votes the necessary two-thirds was lacking. Previously most of us had imagined that the resolution would go through almost *pro forma;* but a great agitation was stirred up by the Hearst papers and by Father Coughlin on the last week-end, which resulted in forty thousand telegrams deluging the United States Senate and the unforseen failure of the resolution. However, that rejection does not vitally affect the World Court. The Court has functioned for a number of years without United States membership. It will continue to function; and, while a gesture of friendship would have been welcome, it was by no means essential. The effect of acceptance and rejection alike was exaggerated by the advocates of the two courses. Had we gone into the World Court we should have made no radical difference, probably no perceptible difference, in its operations. We should have contributed our eighty thousand dollars a year to its expenditures. We should have been under no obligation to use the Court; we should have been bound by none of its decisions. However, these stark facts were denied by the antagonists, who convinced the American people that going into the World Court meant going into the League of Nations; and against going into the League of Nations, we must reluctantly admit, the great majority of the American people still stand.

What are the basic reasons for this attitude of mind of the American public? The American public is not a war-making public; it has a religious fervor for peace probably as intense as animates any people in the world. It is of no avail to argue to our people for going into the League of Nations because war is so wasteful, inhuman, cruel, devilish. Their reply is: "Of course war is all you say; and that's why we won't go into the League of Nations." The objection to going into the League is not because it will prevent war, but because it will bring the United States into war. That is the paradox which we peace-seekers must answer.

What is the reason for this widespread, subconscious, but deep-seated emotion on the part of the citizens of America? It has been evoked by the historical developments of the last two or three years. As a matter of fact, the League of Nations has not succeeded in its main purpose, the prevention of war. It is evident to the people of America that Japan did make war, and that all efforts to curb Japan were futile. It is evident to the people of America that Mussolini dispatched troops to Abyssinia for the purpose of making war. It is evident to the people of America that Abyssinia, a country which is a member of the League, offered to arbitrate, and such arbitration was denied. The League of Nations has not acted with any vigor. Mussolini was given a free hand by France. England was complacent, and an appeal to force instead of an appeal to reason is now going forward.

On Monday night, March 11, 1935, a debate occurred on this subject in the British House of Commons: "Can peace be secured along with security through membership of the League of Nations and the enforcement of its covenant," was asked, "or must the nations fall back upon their old methods of regional pacts and treaties, particularly treaties which amount to alliances, the alliances providing that the forces of all the nations within them shall be instantly used for the defense of each other?" France says, in effect, "The League processes are too slow and cumbersome. They are legal, they are judicial, they call for inquiries, for reports, for multiple conferences, but all the time the aggressor is making war, and it is too late, when all the legal means have been debated and all the compromises considered, to ensure justice and peace. The war by that time has been won or lost; and therefore, we, the government of France, seek alliances which we call pacts of peace, under which we shall be instantly assisted by our allies in case Germany makes war upon us." I have put it concretely. Germany is the possible aggressor France is thinking about all the time.

England, also, has practically come to the same conclusion, although its people are very restless and dissatisfied in submitting to that conclusion. They dislike it intensely, and the Liberal and Labor parties will make an election issue of it next time; but the Conservative party in power secured an indorsement of the House of Commons on March 11th by a majority of 424 to 79. The opposition was practically negligible. On what was that vote taken? It was taken on a resolution which was first couched in criticism of the "white paper" presented by the government two or three weeks earlier, a document which so enraged Hitler that it gave him a bad throat and caused him to retire to his mountain home for consideration of the case. Mr. Stanley Baldwin was very careful, in speaking in the House, to permit no phrase to escape his lips in criticism of or skepticism concerning Chancellor Hitler's illness; but the general European opinion at the time was that the illness was caused by the "white paper", and was an excuse for postponing indefinitely the visit of Sir John Simon, the Foreign Minister, to Berlin. However, that difficulty was overcome and the visit was made, in company with Sir Anthony Eden, who proceeded later to Warsaw and Moscow.

But, for our study, we are particularly concerned with the attitude of the government of England towards the League of Nations and its fundamental purpose, as throwing a light upon the subconscious attitude of the people of the United States, an attitude induced by its daily reading of headlines. Mr. Baldwin said:

"It is not a question in international politics of doing what is ideally best but of doing what is best in the circumstances in which you are. There can be no one who, at the moment, and in the light of the facts of the last two years, can look at the immediate future for the disarmament we hoped could be achieved a few years ago.

"It is difficult to look for complete security in the present state of the League until such time as we hope may come when that system of collective security may be devised. What is left is to try to secure this corner and that in different parts of Europe till you have, as far as you can, put deterrence to any aggressor at any future time."

There is no longer complete confidence in the League processes giving security. Regional arrangements—which is another name for alliances—are to give security in this corner and that until, in the course of time, the League can be strengthened and its guarantees made effective. Sir Austin Chamberlain was more explicit. He said there were two kinds of war, one of them accidental, against which the League offered enormous security. But the other kind, he said is deliberately planned by some country for national aggrandizement or revenge.

"Against such war," he said, "the League, neither now nor in any predictable time, can guarantee protection for a victim of aggression. We can't prevent that kind of war by multiplying pacts or filling up gaps in documents. The only way to prevent that sort of war is to make it clear to a would-be aggressor that such an overwhelming force will be amassed against her that she would have no chance of winning."

Originally it was contemplated that such force, making aggression too great a risk, would be assembled under the ægis of the League of Nations. But no practicable, acceptable scheme for accomplishing that result has been developed, and, as Sir Austin Chamberlain says, "As it stands today, the League is ineffectual in preventing war made by a nation deliberately for national aggrandizement or for revenge."

That is disquieting, disappointing. It will almost break the hearts of some noble, devoted people who have pinned their faith and given their lives for a decade or more to the League of Nations. But to blink the facts would be suicidal; and we in the United States are compelled to recognize that

the conviction of our people respecting the United States joining the League will depend not at all upon what we say, but
upon what member nations do.

England, despite the criticism of the Liberal and Labor
elements, is heavily increasing its air forces; while Germany
has broken the provisions of the Treaty of Versailles. That
treaty forbids the creation of any military or naval air force by
Germany, and yet not only is the air force in existence but it
equals in strength England's air force and has been made an
official arm of the imperial army. England therefore says:
"We have no option. We must arrange our safety against
this possible aggressor. England cannot be left helpless and
stripped." Whether England was previously helpless and
stripped is not for you or me to determine. That is for the
English people to say; but you and I are intensely interested
in their change of mind and attitude. The British government asserts vigorously its continued interest in the League
and its dependence on the League as far as the League can be
made to bear its burden of winning peace and tranquillity.
But, as Sir John Simon said, with the full authority of the
government, "We have come reluctantly to note that the
active membership of the League is not, at present, universal,
and very great difficulties arise if you attempt to put upon
this new international instrument a burden bigger than it can
bear."

So Germany will be challenged either to accept two or
three further steps, or to be faced with what is in effect, although not in terms, an alliance between Italy, France, Belgium, England, and perhaps Holland, against Germany. Germany is challenged to do two or three things: first, return
to the League of Nations. Germany, like Japan, has officially
declared that it does not accept the ideal of the League of
Nations. I have no doubt that, to the average American mind,
which takes general impressions from world events, it appears
extremely curious that any nation that repudiates the objects
of the League of Nations should be implored to return to
membership. The European statesmen say, "We had better

get them inside, and then we can manage them, perhaps." The average American says, "Well, I don't seek their company. I would rather be left out." That is the dilemma in which League advocates are placed.

Next, Germany is required to accept the guarantee of the permanent territorial integrity and independence of Austria. The rest of the nations have made up their minds that the independence and integrity of Austria is essential to the peace of Central Europe and to their own future security. Germany, we know, hankers to draw Austria into its jurisdiction. Third, Germany is asked to enter what is called roughly the Eastern Locarno, which means the mutual guarantee by the countries in the east of Europe—Russia, Poland, Czechoslovakia, Jugoslavia, Roumania—of their respective frontiers.

It is very doubtful whether Germany will enter into that obligation because we know, as a matter of fact, Germany considers Russia the chief enemy. Russia knows that Germany is of that mind, and Russia, while it has become a member of the League of Nations, remits no ounce of effort in building its war machine. So the common man in the United States says: "What is the meaning of membership in the League? Russia is welcomed with great rejoicing. We are assured that its accession strengthens the League immeasurably, but apparently Russia has not the slightest confidence in the League's power to prevent Japan and Germany from attacking it east and west."

This brings us up to the question whether war under these circumstances can be possibly avoided.

Mr. Frank H. Simonds, a writer of indubitable power, one of the brightest and best-informed commentators on world events, in an article on which I have been asked to comment, argues that only through war have oppressed peoples in the past won their liberties and if war be made illegal and impossible, the only means open to win freedom will be denied enslaved peoples.

He overlooks the important fact that the Covenant of the League of Nations does not sanction intervention against a revolutionary war. The Chinese civil war has been raging for over twenty years, most bloody, most devastating, in all its particulars the extreme of abomination; but the League has never contemplated taking any action to stop that war. The Greek revolution of early 1935 was not called to the attention of the League of Nations, because internal war, civil war, is not within the purview of the League. Only international war, war between nations, was the League designed to prevent.

Mr. Simonds goes on to argue that wars will always be waged to win racial unity. He contends that Americans who used war to win their own national unity and independence are inconsistent and visionary when they oppose Germany which proposes to employ war to win its racial unity.

The historic fact is that we Anglo-Saxons do live under a variety of flags. Canada and the United States have not found it essential to come within the same jurisdiction. They have demonstrated that it is practicable for people of the same race to live in harmony side by side under different governments. Germany never did include the Teutons of Czechoslovakia and Switzerland within its domains. Why, then, should the Hitlerites not be criticised when they announce a purpose to bring these groups into their semi-sacred, racial, Teutonic jurisdiction, even at the cost of war?

More important, Mr. Simonds points out that Italy, Germany and Japan threaten war as their only way to procure economic advantages which are essential to their life. Their people are in distress, their economic outlook is black, they cannot sustain their population, he says, unless through war they acquire access to raw materials and to favored markets. Therefore it is not only foolish but also selfish for American Women's Clubs to insist that war for these nations under these conditions is indefensible.

While it must be admitted that each of these three powers labors under circumstances less advantageous than those enjoyed by Great Britain, France and the United States; yet their ambitions are not all dictated by the same motives.

Italy's aim is to reestablish the grandeur and supremacy of the Roman Empire; it asserts primarily, not its need for means of subsistence, but Mussolini's craving for world power and prestige. Germany boasts its purpose to become self-supporting, to establish an autarchy, to embrace all Teutons in its capacious arms, not that they may bring new riches to the Motherland, but that they may rejoice in absorption into the semi-mystical half-divine German brotherhood. Japan, on the other hand, already rules all Japanese, and contemplates with serenity the emigration of its children to Brazil and other sovereignties. Japan seeks primarily exclusive trade rights in China, enforced, if need be, by military subjection of China.

The three militant, peace-disturbing powers have divergent goals. They are alike only in their anachronistic conviction that their purposes can be most advantageously won by war and the threat of war. They announce the precepts of a bygone era. They forget that the twentieth century demands different methods from the eighteenth century, and offers vastly improved means of life.

It is true that Germany, Italy and Japan are handicapped by having come, full-panoplied, late upon the international scene. There remain few new regions to occupy by European methods, few sources of raw materials and lands for colonization which have not been pre-empted. But, in part compensation, these powers enjoy scientific and machine means of producing wealth that their sister nations have no more than they enjoyed in earlier decades.

Italy has increased its national wealth more by "The battle of the wheat", enlarging the area and increasing the yield of the wheat crop, than it ever can by terrorizing or fighting Abyssinia. By developing its water powers and becoming partially independent of outside purchases of coal, Italy can improve its home manufactures and supply its own people with machine goods without seeking vainly for Italian-owned overseas coal supplies. Nations, like individuals, have "acres of diamonds" waiting to be uncovered on their native soils.

Germany made a cardinal error, perhaps, when it expended tens of millions of dollars, (borrowed abroad and not likely to be repaid), in the decade after the war, in reorganizing and modernizing its industrial system in preparation for mass production in the American style. Mass production called for mass export. But all the industrial nations could not simultaneously expand their world sales of standardized goods. So Germany sank deep in the industrial depression. The owners of the idle mills, and mines, and factories, and chemical works, feverishly search abroad for outlets. But Hitler preaches self-sufficiency. The two ideals conflict. Neither is wholly attainable; but self-support as an ideal has the advantage of not needing war to further it.

However, the equipment of the new conscript army along with the construction of barracks, forts and military roads, big guns and airplanes, has boomed the heavy industries temporarily; but the full employment of the immense manufacturing facilities permanently must necessitate foreign markets.

Can foreign markets be won by war? Already the Russian market has been contracted by the threat of an attack on the Ukraine and by Hitler's repeated declaration: "Communism is the enemy." Eastern Europe might be opened to German economic penetration if Germany supported vigorously, in friendship with the Little Entente, a Danubian customs union. But Hitler's avowed purpose to force Austria, and parts of Czechoslovakia to come under his rule shuts the tighter the borders of the Danubian lands against German goods. As for Asia and Africa—can Germany be so mad as to try to blast open their markets with big guns and bombing planes? No. War is not a good sales agent. Germany dedicated in reality to peaceful intercourse with its neighbours would find more customers than Germany rattling the sabre and yelling defiance.

Japan, the third of the powers to which, it is argued, war may be a beneficial necessity, is finding by experience in China that bayonets may be countered by boycotts. Japan is truly hard pressed to sustain its increasing population on the overpeopled home islands. It seeks to imitate British methods.

It aims to make China in the twentieth century serve Japan as India in the nineteenth century served Britain. But, the conditions are markedly different, and different centuries call for different ways. Japan has conquered in Manchuria; because Manchuria was an outlying province of China which had never been more than a semi-independent satrapy, a pioneer land only recently brought under partial cultivation by settlers from south of the Great Wall. Japan may reap some commercial profit and official gains by administering Manchuria. The nations of the world, including the United States, may be brought to renounce the Stimson doctrine of non-recognition of Manchuria, and the Japanese military party may be able to point to success in Manchuria in support of their claim that war is profitable.

But China proper, where for centuries the Chinese emperors have ruled, where every inch of land is cultivated by a population staggeringly industrious and thrifty, where armies of over two million soldiers well equipped fight under the orders of Nanking, where Japan is hated more than any other foreign power and where the sentiment of nationality has been fervidly cultivated by the teachings of the revered leader Sun Yat Sen—China may prove the grave of Japanese ambition. A friendly China might be an El Dorado for Japanese merchants. A hostile China could never be subjugated as India and Manchuria were subjugated, nor be made to yield rich returns to a conqueror.

Italy, Germany, Japan, all three, may keep the world on tenter-hooks; may struggle to gain economic advantage by force; but they will only demonstrate anew that in a world of science and machines and trade, war is a vestigal survival of barbarism and does not pay.

However, for the United States the crucial point is that Japan is convinced today that by dominating China the home economic situation will be permanently relieved. And Japan must be met upon that issue if she is to be met at all.

That brings us to the problems which intimately concern the United States. Suppose we accept the verdict, for the present, that the United States shall not be urged to accept full membership of the League of Nations, suppose we admit that to attack the opponent on that front is to attack him on his strongest side. Suppose we take a lesson from the shrewdest of warriors and try to get round the strongest line of the foe, instead of butting head-on into his impregnable fortresses. Have we then open to us any fruitful line of activity? I am sure we have. That line of activity has been developed by the Hoover and Roosevelt administrations and, to some extent, by previous administrations. We should not be disheartened as friends of the League, for in point of fact, we are in the League of Nations in almost everything except name. The United States has been cooperating intensively for years in every movement which directly concerned the organization and the maintenance of the peace of the world. Some of our citizens are afraid that, if we formally accept full membership, we may become embroiled in many questions which do not directly affect the maintenance of peace; but wherever there arises a matter which does concern the organization and the strengthening of the peace of the world, the United States is already just as active as it might be with full membership. For instance, just at the time when the Senate was rejecting membership of the World Court there was before the Disarmament Commission a full treaty submitted by the United States for consideration and adoption, which provided for the inspection and control by an international commission of the manufacture and sale, and particularly the export, of munitions of war in all countries. The submission of that treaty, its support, vigorous and continuous, by the United States delegates, is more directly important for the future peace of the world than even the United States' membership of the World Court. For that treaty means action; it means our leadership in the assertion of the international interest in munitions-making and export, and our willingness to have a commission under the Secretariat of the League of Nations visit the United States as well as all other countries, to ensure that the provisions of the treaty are being strictly obeyed.

While the Senate was debating the World Court the decision was rendered on the case of *I'm Alone*, the Canadian freighter which was sunk far outside the twenty-mile limit by an American customs rumboat chaser. Had the sinking of the rum-runner and the drowning of a sailor occurred in European waters and, say, Greek and Turkish vessels been involved, a war scare would possibly have been raised. But, fortunately, so ingrained is the conviction in Canada and the United States that such disputes shall be determined judicially that a court of arbitration, composed of a member of the highest tribunal in each country, was accepted by both sides and proceeded to adjudication. So quietly and as a matter of routine were all the proceedings conducted that, not until the verdict was rendered, was the public conscious of them. The United States was adjudged liable to damages. Without a second thought the verdict was cheerfully accepted, the damages paid and the controversy finished.

Thus was a new demonstration made of the American policy of judicial settlement of international, judiciable disputes. It is noteworthy that the matter was referred neither to the International Court of Arbitration at the Hague, nor to the World Court, but to an *ad hoc* tribunal. But the paramount fact is that judicial determination was prompt and decisive.

Our line of action should be to strengthen the United States government in its endeavors to find opportunities for cooperating with the League in matters that actually concern the peace of the world. We can be content, as I see it, to leave the United States free from any complicity in the fate of Austria. Whether Austria should be joined to Germany or remain independent is none of our business and is not a question in which we want to intervene. We can be well content to leave our hands free in the multitude of matters constantly under discussion in the chancelleries of Europe which concern exclusively their relations with each other, relations which change so rapidly that even a student can hardly keep track of them. We always contended, we supporters of the League, that membership would not involve us, of necessity, in the political concerns of other nations; but the activities of the members of the League and the continual embroilment of the League in political concerns, the multiplicity of pacts which, for example, they are now concluding over Europe, indicate to the average American citizen that there is no such complete severance between political matters and peace matters. So long as we take an active part in peace matters we are doing our share in fulfilling the original purpose.

Two peace problems of serious weight are permanently our concern. "Peace," as General Smuts said, "is more threatened in the Pacific Ocean than in any other part of the world," and in that situation we are involved. We have undertaken special relations with Japan and China which involve us of necessity, inescapably, in the problems of the western Pacific. Our preparedness for peace must be directed chiefly towards those problems and they are urgent, immediate; they challenge the American people.

What are the two doctrines which involve us? First, the doctrine of the territorial integrity and political independence of China; second, the doctrine of neutral rights on the seas in time of war. Look at these briefly. We have entered into a nine-power treaty which declares that to us the territorial integrity of China is a matter of special concern and that, with the other signatories of the treaty, we will maintain that integrity. Japan has not the slightest intention of abiding by the terms of that treaty. Are we going to assert that our interests in China are so vital and extensive that we will face even a war with Japan to maintain those interests? That is a question which, within the next year or two, America will have to answer, and it is for us peace-seekers at once to explore that problem and try to solve it.

We are building a navy up to treaty strength. We have the excuse, the justification, that we made a treaty in 1930 and that we are abiding by that treaty. Nothing that we are doing goes beyond that treaty. But the type of navy which we are building puts Japan on notice that it is meant for fighting, not in home waters, but in the western Pacific Ocean. America insists on building post-Jutland dreadnoughts of 35,000 tons burden and cruisers of 10,000 tons carrying eight-inch guns, because smaller vessels would not have a cruising range long enough to carry them across the ocean and back. A war with Japan in Japanese Pacific waters is indicated. Our navy officials would admit that assumption and the people of our Pacific coast would not only admit it but demand it. Our navy will hold great maneuvers in the Pacific in the summer of 1935. A roster of persons in church and educational life have presented a petition to the United States president, asking him not to permit those maneuvers to be carried out in the Pacific Ocean, because they will give offense to Japan. The situation is so delicate, so acute, that even the normal use of the navy in time of peace to practise evolutions and to fit itself for the performance of its duties is regarded as menacing.

So we are driven to go beneath the surface and ask: "Are we going to insist that Japan shall not acquire dominance in China?" Our interests in that semi-continent are relatively small. British interests far exceed them. British statesmen, like Lord Lothian and General Smuts assume that our policy is fixed and immutable; and that we shall not permit China to be brought under the rule of Japan or divided among the other powers. Is the policy immutable? That is for you and me and the rest of our citizens to determine. Perhaps to aid us in making the decision we shall demand a scientific enquiry, which has never yet been made, into the credits and debits of our trade with China and of all our interests in the western Pacific. I expect that, if such a scientific enquiry be made, it will be found that our trade with China costs us more than it brings. The profits are paid to the traders; the costs are largely met by the taxpayers. The taxpayers are scarcely conscious that they pay for the defence of China trade, by gunboats that patrol the Yangtse and other rivers and fleet units stationed at Shanghai and in Pacific waters. The few individuals and corporations that reap a profit (though they also find that profit by no means sure) may wish to be unyielding to Japan; but the taxpayers who pay the national overhead may wonder whether the prestige is worth the cost.

First, then, we have to determine whether the doctrine of the open door and of the territorial integrity of China which was laid down in 1900 and was endorsed and made formal and binding in 1922, is to remain a fundamental part of the United States foreign policy.

Mr. T. A. Bissom, in the Foreign Policy Bulletin of March 29, 1935, bluntly states: "The most effective American peace policy would be unequivocal withdrawal from the Far East. Such a policy would require complete severing of Philippine ties, a determination not to back up the open door policy by force, the relinquishment of American extraterritorial privileges in China, and the withdrawal of American troops and gunboats from that country. The costs of this policy must be faced and accepted if the dangerous drift of events in the Far East is to be brought under control."

Even if, by taking a realistic view of the situation, we keep out of war directly declared between the United States and Japan, we may be drawn into a war with Japan on another issue, the second which challenges the attention of the peace societies,—the doctrine of neutral rights in time of war.

Japan and Russia may go to war with each other at any time; at least, that is the opinion of most of the chancelleries of the world. Russia is anxious to avoid war; but the military party in Japan has a long-time scheme of Asiatic expansion. Suppose war should supervene, despite all efforts to negotiate. How would American interests be menaced? International trade, its promotion, its expansion, its protection has been the one continuing aim, since the beginning, of American foreign policy. That factor led through the 18th and 19th centuries to the declaration of so-called "neutral rights in warfare." The assertion of these rights has several times brought the United States near to war and two or three times has pulled the United States into war. Mr. Charles Warren, attorney in the State Department in charge of enforcing neutral rights during the war, has written articles developing the dangers under which we stand. As a matter of fact, not a single one of the issues with which we came into disagreement, first with the Allies, and second with Germany; not one of the naval issues which did, in fact, bring us into war with Germany has yet been settled. All the questions in dispute about submarine warfare, about taking passengers and crew from sinking vessels, about the right of the United States to navigate the seas without disturbance from extensive mine fields, about freedom of commerce with belligerents, every one of them stands unchanged. If, against a naval power like Japan, we should assert those rights, when Japan and Rusisa were at war, Mr. Warren's considered opinion is that the United States would inevitably be drawn into the fight. And there is no higher authority.

The State Department has drafted a number of bills to be presented to the Senate on some aspects of the subject, as soon as the Senate has a little time to take up matters not entirely domestic. But the action of the State Department will depend in large part upon the diffused opinion of the American people. Now Mr. Warren says, "The assertion of rights is in itself an offensive action." If a right is asserted, immediately the back is hunched and the fist clenched. So the whole question of neutral rights, which has been probably the most persistent part of American foreign policy, should be reconsidered. American citizens can profitably consider it and come to a determination about it. It is up to us.

Imagine Russia and Japan at war. Russia depends upon its air force for its defense. It has around Vladivostock a number of squadrons of bombing planes. It hopes to bomb the cities of Japan. Japan will immediately take measures, naturally, in case of war, to have these planes destroyed. Russia will immediately place with the United States big orders for airplanes and airplane parts. Airplanes and airplane parts have never been officially recognized as munitions of war; therefore there is no international law against their transportation to Russia. Japan will protest. Japan will seize the ships carrying airplanes and airplane parts. Japan will sink the ships. Japan will say, "That is invaluable aid to the enemy which American citizens are giving." American citizens, stimulated by the yellow press, will howl for the immediate despatch of the American fleet to Japanese waters to protect these ships. Then the fat will be in the fire. Preparedness for peace requires that we members of peace organizations in the United States shall immediately direct our attention to that question. Great Britain has been pleading with the United States periodically since the war for a revision of the laws of neutrality. The United States Senate sees no reason for coming to any agreement with anybody as to how we shall act at a future time; but nothing is more dangerous than to drift on this question. If the people themselves are stirred the United States State Department will accept the decision of the people and will act. It is more important for the future peace of the United States that we shall solve the question of neutral rights in time of war than that we shall go into the League of Nations.

That is our problem. It is not Europe's. It is not the League's. I imagine that the old sea dogs in the British Admiralty are chortling when they see the United States being "put up against it" by Japan. Our State Department has been hoping and thinking that this is only a question between us and Great Britain; and we need be in no hurry to make any concessions to Great Britain. But it isn't between us and Great Britain any longer. It is between us and Japan. Once war is started, any concessions on our part become trebly difficult. Done now in the piping times of peace, we can make scientific, objective conclusions as to what really are the interests of the United States. So to that problem we must give our attention. Here are now opportunities for peace preparedness valuable in the extreme. We endorse Jefferson's motto, "Peace, commerce, and friendship with all nations"; but we find that sometimes commerce conflicts with friendship, and sometimes commerce shatters peace. The first of that trilogy in Jefferson's statement was "peace"; the second was "commerce".

81

We shall be asked to reverse the order, and put the interests of commerce prior to the interests of peace. It is for us, the American people to assert: "No, we stand by the order laid down by Jefferson; first peace, then commerce, and peace and commerce will fructify in friendship."

PART II

❖

THREE DICTATORSHIPS AND THREE DEMOCRACIES

*The Foundations of Their Domestic
and Foreign Relations*

CHAPTER V

Russia

and

Communism

CHAPTER V

Russia and Communism

I HAVE in my hand a translation of the report made by Stalin, the boss dictator of Russia, early in 1934 to the all-Soviet conference of the Communist Party. He winds up that report by shouting, "Long live the invincible banner of Marx, Engels, and Lenin!" Who are these three who compose the triune deity of the rulers of 168 million people occupying one-sixth of the world's occupied area?

Of Lenin you have heard: the short, homely leader who was exiled from Russia after starting revolutionary movements; who had been sent to Siberia, had escaped, and wandered from capital to capital in Europe; who, at the outbreak of the World War, was in Switzerland, and who from thence was conveyed with the approval of the German general staff in a sealed car with various of his assoicates across Germany, that he might land safe in Petersburg and from there start a fire behind the Russian lines which would give victory to the German forces—Lenin, the conquering revolutionist.

Of Karl Marx some of you have heard, Marx, the theoretical founder of modern Socialism. Karl Marx was born in Germany of a line of Jewish rabbis. He was educated as a Protestant. He attended the German universities. He wrote revolutionary articles in German newspapers. He was harried, in the early forties of the nineteenth century, out of Germany into Paris and into London. There he met the third of these three divinities of Russia, Frederick Engels.

Engels was the son of a rich manufacturer who had factories in both England and Germany. Engels had had the advantage of the best English education. He was already a Communist before he met Karl Marx. They formed an alliance, and in union they wrote, in 1848, the "Communist Manifesto", possibly the most effective propagandist document ever written. It begins: "A spectre is haunting Europe—the spectre of Communism. All the powers of old Europe have entered into a holy alliance to exorcise this spectre. Pope and Czar, Metternich and Guizot, French radicals and German police-spies." And it concludes, after a passionate portrayal of European and world history, informed with great learning and heated with earnest conviction: "The Communists disdain to conceal their views and their aims. They openly declare that their ends can be attained only by the forcible overthrow of all existing social conditions. May the ruling classes tremble at a Communist revolution! The proletarians have nothing to lose but their chains. They have a world to gain. Working men of all countries, unite!"

That has been the slogan of the Communists in all countries ever since. The revolution which immediately broke out in 1848 in various European countries was the most disappointing of failures that revolutionists have ever encountered. But Marx and Engels continued with their intellectual work and with attempts, feeble and largely futile, at revolutionary organization.

Marx in London lived at first in direst poverty. He had married a refined aristocratic German lady. When one of their children died, she had to go around the corner and beg from a French refugee the ten dollars needed to buy the coffin. Always they were harried with debt. Sheriffs and duns were their daily persecutors. Marx earned a few pounds by newspaper work, oddly enough in large part for the New York *Tribune*. Later Engels generously subsidized him. He proceeded to write what has become the scriptures of Russia, the great learned work called Das Kapital, the work to which the Russians and the Communists appeal as the fundamentalists appeal to the Holy Scriptures. If any action can be defended by the quotation of paragraphs from Das Kapital or from a work by Engels, that action is justified. Until the outbreak of the Bolshevist revolution, these Communist scriptures were known to few. George Bernard Shaw and I devoted a winter in the nineties to reading the first volume, which was alone published at that time, he in the British Museum and I in a library in East London. My wife at the same period had organized a class in New York which met through the winter to listen to an erudite Russian refugee, who had been a professor at Chicago, elucidate to their highly tutored female minds the abstrusities of the Communist scriptures. We were exceptions.

But when the Bolsheviks came into power the whole world awoke to the fiery significance of Engels and Marx; and now whole libraries have been written in exposition, confirmation, or condemnation of these doctrines. I met Engels in his extreme old age at Zurich in the middle of the Gay Nineties, when I attended, with Shaw and others, an international Socialist conference summoned by the Second Internationale. The first afternoon I had an amusing illustration of the narrow fanaticism provoked in the Marxists of the straiter sects. We met on the street Harry Quelch, who was a member of a small, unimportant, but highly self-conscious group of Marxian Socialists in England. Shaw held out his hand in greeting and Quelch ostentatiously hid his hands behind his back. He would not shake the hand of a Socialist who was also humorous and who could see the folly and the comical aspects of the veneration, the adoration of Karl Marx. At the meetings the platform was decorated with a great painting of Marx over the wall in the rear, adorned with whiskers of Russian amplitude. We English Fabians scoffed and jeered at the continental Socialists who were almost prepared to bow down before that portrait as if it were an icon.

However, undoubtedly Marx's works supplied the foundation, intellectual and scientific, of modern Socialism. Up to that time Socialism had been a sentimental movement without intellectual underpinnings. You have seen, many of you, the picture of Tolstoi's "Resurrection", *Do We Live Again?* You remember the hero is a landowner who announces loudly at the opening to the maid who is to become his victim that all lands should belong to the people, and, how, after a period of debauchery, his conscience awakes and he demonstrates his reformation in part by distributing his land among his peasants. That was Tolstoi's Christian version of Socialism,—a personal reformation resulting in a personal sacrifice. Karl Marx and the Communists pooh-poohed that teaching because, they said: "It can never result in any radical social change. The appeal to love and to the sense of justice of the powerful and the rulers cannot bring a new world to the oppressed."

Marx elaborated several fundamental doctrines. We will consider the most important of them in order and examine the application of these doctrines in Russia; first, to domestic affairs, and at the end of the lecture, to international affairs. The three doctrines we will consider are: the Economic Interpretation of History; the Doctrine of Surplus Value; and the Doctrine of Class War.

First, the Economic Interpretation of History. Marx and Engels and Lenin contend that all great historic movements have been the outcome of the economic system, the method by which people were making a living. They deny that morals or religion or nationalism played any important or controlling part in any great historic changes. They contend, for instance, that the abolition of slavery in the United States was purely the result of the fact that slavery no longer paid. In the North, they contend, it was evident that slave labor was much less profitable by the sixties and the fifties than free labor, and in the South the planters were working against the tide of time in opposing the abolition of slavery, and they were defeated because they didn't recognize economic conditions. If they had been wise they would have seen that it was to their interest, also, as well as to the Northerners to substitute free labor at wages for slave labor at subsistence costs. All religion, morality, culture, education are the emanations of the economic system, the system thought out and expressed by the rulers for the buttressing of their authority and power, for the maintenance of their economic privileges. And therefore, when the Bolshevists came to power, they opposed religion, all religion, as the opiate of the people, the drug administered by the bourgeoisie to the downtrodden peasants and proletarians to keep them quiet while they were being plundered. It is not only or mainly that the Greek Orthodox church was corrupt, ignorant, superstitious; it is not that Rasputin acquired a malignant power, through his mummeries, with the Czar's wife and family, it is not that the local priests were undeserving of respect for either their intellectual attainments or their moral practices; it is that religion is of necessity the expression of the dominant system of economic organization. The Protestants, who had organized welfare churches, who were modernized in their beliefs and practices, were equally condemned by the Bolshevists, because their own scripture taught that all religion is the opiate of the people.

Similarly with morals. All morals are the outcome of the experiences in the economic life and are directed to the strengthening of the dominant economic class. And so the Bolshevists practically destroyed the old moral edifice. They declared sex freedom, for sex practices, marriage, and divorce are also the emanations of the economic system and, since the old bourgeois system was to be abolished, its moral life, its code of commandments must also be abolished and free ground be left for the development of a new moral order, the emanation of the new, the more glorious economic life which was to be established,—which is now being established. The first excesses which arose so soon as the old restraints were abandoned are being fast curtailed. A new moral obligation is being taught and enforced. But that moral obligation is being based on allegiance to the Socialist and Communist State. The men and women who are loose in their sex relations are being banned, ostracised. A perfectly puritanical demand is made upon the members of the favored Communist Party. Within a week or two punishment has been meted out in the faraway corner of Asia against a man who had married seven wives in nine months and had collected the wages due the seven wives and then divorced the lot. Stalin and the leaders, in their fervid support of their new Jerusalem, lead ascetic lives and slowly—well, not so slowly, either—and surely order, abstinence, discipline, self-control are being established, not on the basis of obedience to God or his commandments, but on the basis of the welfare of the Soviet State.

All culture must have the same basis. At first the writings and the plays and the novels and the poems all harped on one string—the Bolshevist doctrines; but lately the Trade Union of Writers has been admonished that some art is desirable in artistic work, and that sound theology is no substitute for bad workmanship. In that also the change is accelerating. Thus the working out of this doctrine—doctrine very imperfectly true—of the economic basis of history is developed.

The next doctrine we shall consider is that of Surplus Value, a doctrine demonstrably incorrect. It so happened that Marx wrote and Engels wrote in the forties in England, which were one of the darkest decades in British history, blighted by the unchecked pursuit of profit by factory owners who had as yet not been brought under any governmental control or checked by an enlightened public opinion. Engels wrote an account of the English working classes in the forties which makes one shudder. And these conditions were the basis of Karl Marx's argumentation. He said that all wage earners are exploited, that the factory owner, personal or corporate, robs the workman regularly by taking from him the difference between what the commodity costs in raw material and what the commodity is sold for in the market. He made no allowances for taxes and overhead as we style it, but he just subtracted cost of raw material and selling price and said the difference, after you have paid the wages, is the exploitation of the laborer. He was himself, as Bertrand Russell points out, at the moment benefiting in the British Museum from the expenditure of national taxes, but he made no allowance for that item in the costs of manufacturing. However, what is important is that he gave a pseudo-scientific air to the indisputable truth that the wage-earner was receiving collectively less than might have been given him, less than subsequent factory acts and trade union movements and social re-

94

form agencies procured for him. But the message has been, "You workmen, you are all being robbed daily. Your wage envelope could be filled far fuller," and "You men unite and rise against this exploitation." The world he divided into two classes, the bourgeoisie and the proletariat. The bourgeoisie are all those who obtain any income, even five dollars, except from wages and salaries. The proletariat are those who have no source of income except wages and salaries. "Bourgeois" is the fellest epithet in the Communist vocabulary. Stalin repeatedly in this document in my hand refers to his opponents as "Bourgeois rightists", and they are *ipso facto* under condemnation.

The cure for this burglarious condition is the acquiring of all productive machinery, land, factories, machine shops, works, stores—everything that is utilized in the production and distribution of wealth—by the State. So the Bolshevists immediately devoted themselves to the overthrow of all private ownership in the means of production, distribution, and exchange. In the means of factory and workshop production, that was relatively easy; for, after the victory of a bloody revolution the owners were helpless, and it simply meant taking over their property and declaring it to be State-owned. They have gone ahead with the construction of other great industrial properties most successfully. Unquestionably the Bolshevists have industrialized Russia. They have demonstrated that government in business and government forming the whole of business can be worked, worked with many defects, worked with much suffering, but still worked. Stalin himself catalogues their deficiencies, their errors, their blunders, their lapses, with a thoroughness which no hostile economist could excel. He tells of the bureaucratic spirit, of the lack of initiative, of the want of personal interest, of everything that has been predicted as an accompaniment of huge government enterprises. But he tells the faults that the Communist Party may rectify them. Their Five-Year Plan wasn't anything like the success that was first declared. They have caught up now, several years later, with the production of the heavy industries which they set as their goal. Their distribution is terribly poor. Within a week or two an official publication has told of a man who went all over Russia looking for a suit of clothes, a lamp, and a water bucket. It is a fact that in Russian cities it is still impossible to purchase a thread and needles or thimble, or any one of the multitude of articles which fill our five-and-ten-cents stores and our drug stores. We shall see that the peasants complain that for the sacrifices they have made they are not able to obtain food and clothes and tea and sugar.

But the newest investigations report a considerable improvement in that respect, and Stalin calls ever and anon some fresh division of that select corps, the Communist Party, to remedy these abuses. We shall await with eagerness the outcome of his efforts. Unemployment, he says, has been abolished, whereas, in capitalist countries like the United States, millions rove the streets with no work for their hands to do. That is true. Mr. Henry S. Chamberlin, the *Christian Science Monitor* correspondent, says it would be more accurate, perhaps, to say that there is forced labor, no unemployment but compulsory employment. Slaves were not unemployed ever, he remarks, and now in Russia the proletarians have no choice but to accept the job that's offered them or to suffer the sacrifice of their bread cards and face almost certain starvation. You can make your choice. Is it better to wander the streets with no work to do and no wages coming in, with the wife and children sobbing and starving at home, or to be offered a job on the condition that if you don't take that job, then you will be left to starve?

The last doctrine—let's see, we have had the Economic Interpretation of History; we have had the Doctrine of Surplus Value—the last one is the Doctrine of the Class War, and this deals with the methods of establishing and maintaining Communism. You will read that the aim of Communism is to establish a classless society. By that they mean not that there will be no differences between skilled and unskilled workers and technical scientists, between the heads of the government and the lowest stenographer in a public office; they mean only that this great division into two classes, the bourgeoisie and the proletariat, will be effaced; no longer will some live in idleness and others live by work. That doctrine leads them to their cruelties, to their implacable overthrow of opposing classes. In agriculture they found that the peasant didn't want to throw his farm into a common State pool. He wanted to work his farm individually, to own it for his very own. But this was contrary to the teachings of Karl Marx and Engels and Lenin, and so a fearsome compulsory collectivization of farms was established, and great Soviet farms grew up, State-owned. The collectives were theoretically cooperatively owned, the State farms and the collective farms were governmentally owned. Stalin says that these Soviet farms have been so far a flat economic failure, and he calls for radical changes in their organization, the breaking up into smaller units, the establishment of diversity, and so on. The kulaks, the prosperous peasants who were liquidated, were the heaviest sufferers. Liquidation meant exile, starvation, death. It is impossible to forgive the ruthless, inhuman cruelty of these professors of a higher humanity to the well-to-do and even the poor peasants. Last year I told you that two million had died in the government-made famine of the previous winter and spring. I was conservative. Mr. Chamberlin demonstrates that the deaths must have reached four millions, a terrible toll to pay for the establishment of any prospective paradise.

Skepticism about the accuracy of Mr. Chamberlin's figures and of his trustworthiness as a reporter on Russia has been expressed. "How is it possible," has been asked, "that so terrible a famine ravaged Russia and that resident correspondents, such as Mr. Walter Duranty, of the New York *Times*, and Mr. Louis Fischer of the New York *Nation*, did not fully report it?" That is a pertinent question and Mr. Chamberlin answers it.

He explains that in early 1933, while the effects of the famine were most dire and widespread, the "censorship in

Moscow was greatly aided by a new ruling under which correspondents might not leave Moscow without submitting a detailed itinerary and obtaining special travel permission from the Commissariat for Foreign Affairs. Permissions were systematically withheld when it was a question of traveling in the rural regions of Ukraine and the North Caucasus"—two of the most afflicted famine areas. "It was only with considerable difficulty that the sole French correspondent in Moscow obtained permission to meet M. Herriot, arriving on a goodwill tour in Odessa. The correspondent was strictly forbidden to stray off the route which had been marked out for Herriot and his party, from which, naturally, all unpleasant traces of famine had been carefully removed." Thus the story of the famine was effectively "killed."

Mr. Chamberlin relates in detail his own enquiry in the autumn, when a favorable new harvest had been reaped.

He visited three districts, and found an appalling deterioration in the physical conditions of regions which had been among the most fertile in Russia. In the first household he entered at random there had been seven victims. In one of the larger Cossack villages the head of the local Soviet assured him, in rebuttal of exaggerated statements by peasants, that "on the basis of our official figures only 850 died out of a former population of 8000"—ten per cent.

In Poltava the maid in the hotel "burst out with a vivid and quite unsolicited account of the terrible scenes which the town had lived through during the winter and spring; dying children clinging to dead parents; carts making their rounds and picking up the corpses lying in the streets." She may have been hysterical; but her testimony "was confirmed by scores of people with whom I talked in the town and in the surrounding villages."

In the sugar beet country, west of the Dnieper, one village, the worst sufferer found reported, through the secretary of the local Soviet, that 600 of the 2000 inhabitants had perished—thirty per cent.

Summing up the results, after allowing for the normal

mortality, this experienced reporter, the only one who claims himself to have gone and seen and counted, estimates that ten per cent of the population in the stricken districts died of famine and of the diseases which followed famine, typhus, influenza and other afflictions. Of forty million people ten per cent is four million.

What caused this frightful calamity? Partly the determined, obstinate resistance of the peasants to the new collective farms and to the excessive requisitions of previous years; partly the cruel and relentless collections made by local Bolshevist officials during the time of stringency, collections from which the peasants tearfully and continuously begged relief; and partly the drought which blasted large areas.

Mr. Maurice Hindus, an American enquirer above suspicion of bias, corroborates Mr. Chamberlin's account of the peaceful resistance of the peasants during the autumn of 1932 and the condition of the fields, overgrown with weeds, utterly neglected, hardly worth reaping, that resulted from their sullen, hopeless lying-down on the job. He also endorses the story of the far wandering of villagers during the food-shortage in search of rye and wheat and of the frightful reduction in the number of horses, cattle and sheep, and testifies that the central government did not bestir itself till too late. He explains that the Moscow authorities exacted the penalty of death from some of the local leaders for their blundering, their cruelty, their false reports. But, as he says, the execution of guilty Communists did not bring back to life the millions of dead cattle; nor, we can add, the other more pitiful millions of dead women and children.

Had free enquiry and report on the conditions been encouraged it is possible that the central power might have alleviated the hunger and misery. But they were angry with the farmers for their mass opposition to the vast changes on which Stalin insisted and they were willing, so long as they were not fully aware of the appalling facts, to let the peasant suffer for his recalcitrance. The President of the Poltava District Soviet Executive Committee said, slowly and deliberately, to Mr.

Chamberlin: "To have imported grain from abroad would have been injurious to our prestige. To have relaxed the requisitions would have meant that the peasants would never have worked again, because they would have always expected the Government to come to their aid. The Government went on the path which it chose consciously."

The whole sad story is an example of the magnitude of the consequences that follow from a major error when a vast country is subject to a centralized dictatorship; when, for the multiplicity of small blunders possible under individualism is substituted the single big blunder, spread over the country, not remediable by individuals or groups, which may decimate a people like an act of God.

Good harvests in later years and more considerate treatment of the peasants have reconciled most of them to the collective farming, mitigated, as it now is, by the private control of small patches of land and of a few cattle and poultry, which gives both incentive and sustenance to separate families.

The greatest triumph of the Soviets has been in the realm of education. There they have conquered more swiftly, more thoroughly, and on a more widespread scale than has any other country in the world in a similarly short period. Their doctrine is: the mighty shall be brought low, and they that are humble shall be exalted, and so their special clients and favorites are the children of the working classes. To these they have extended education which has now become universally compulsory and generously State-supported. The lower, the middle, and the higher schools have multiplied rapidly. The scientific institutions devoted to original research were doubled in four years. The pre-school care of children in kindergartens and *creches* reached eight hundred thousand at the beginning of the period, and nearly six millions at the end of the period reported on last year. We in America are devoted to education, but the self-sacrificing and earnest devotion of the Russians put even us to shame.

Were they in charge of Winter Park, drastic metamorphosis would occur in that regard. Very soon the restriction of education for the Negro proletariat to one-sixth or one-twelfth per head of the amounts given for white education would be reversed. Rollins College would be handed over to the colored people. The white aristocrats, who now live luxuriously, according to Russian standard, in its dormitories, would be given a heavy dose of the treatment that has been meted out to the unprivileged and oppressed former slave class.

To comprehend them we should need an earthquake to shake up our own mental processes. The most reprehensible feature has been their denial of education, especially in the higher schools, to the children of the former privileged classes; for the Lord thy God Marx is a jealous God, visiting the sins of the fathers on the children to the third and fourth generation. Marx wrote the Old Testament of Socialism. And this doctrine has been enforced with relentless severity, now moderating as they grow more secure.

It looked a few months ago as if the OGPU, the agent of the tyranny against all classes, was being stripped of some of its power, but on December first, in Petrograd, one of the Big Ten of the Communist Party was shot dead by a comrade. Immediately the ruthlessness was restored. One hundred and seventy were executed. Arrests proceeded hither and yon, and last week two of the old leaders, Zinoviev and Kamenef, were arrested and tried, tried not for open acts, but for heresy. The state paper gave out that their offense was that they *believed* that Stalin was restoring a personal dictatorship, they *believed* that the statements given out as to the progress of the Five-Year Plan were a deliberate misleading of the proletariat, they *believed* that the workman was getting worse off instead of better off, they *believed* that Stalin was false to the scriptures by abstaining from international agitation, and so on. They have been sentenced for this heresy to ten- and five-years imprisonment respectively. Stalin, although he is only the secretary of the Communist Party, sits supreme in the land, as the boss of one of our political parties—in Philadelphia, the Republicans, in New York the Democratic Party —sits supreme, during his tenure of office, over the whole of his party membership.

That brings me to what I must hastily review—and I have omitted a great deal which I hoped to have time to say—to a consideration of Russian international policies. To comprehend them we must understand that the foreign policy of Russia is based on a fundamentally different conception from the basis of the foreign policy of capitalist countries. To Russians the world is divided into bourgeois and proletariat. The proletariat are their friends; the bourgeoisie of all countries are their enemies. Workers of the World, Unite! Engels wrote, "The workers of all countries have one interest, they have one enemy to fight, they have one prospective victory to win." And so it is not as Germans or as British or as Americans that they array themselves against other peoples. They say, "We deny any interest whatever in national, religious, racial, or color divisions." They have given complete national freedom to the variegated nationalists that make up the Socialist Soviet Republics. They abhor anti-semitism. To them a white man is no more sacred than a black man or a yellow man. They try to make their foreign policy demonstrate that they have no hostility to foreigners as such, but only to the governing classes in the foreign countries who represent, as they say, the capitalist interests. They scoff at pacifism. Stalin speaks of "bourgeois pacifism in its last throes", because they say that you can't have peace so long as you have the inner conflict in each country, between bourgeois and proletariat.

It is one of the paradoxes of history that in countries outside Europe Socialists and Communists, who must be kept distinct in mind, always oppose military preparedness in their home countries. The Socialist Party in this country came near a split last spring because one faction wanted to declare the policy of the party to be that under no circumstances would they take part in a future war. The extreme pacifist, as I have been asked to explain, is one who takes the position: "I will not fight for King and Country", as the boys at Oxford resolved; or, less extreme, "I will devote my whole effort to the avoidance of war and to the removal of all causes of war, in which I class increased armaments as a chief." Those of us who support vigorously the organization of institutions for the prevention of war, while maintaining a reasonable self-defense by our own army and naval forces, Stalin calls "bourgeois pacifists". The Red Army is the pet of the nation, the strongest, best equipped, best trained military force, perhaps, in the world today. The Soviet governments have distorted their domestic procedures on account of their terror of attack from without. They have been convinced that the capitalist world envied them their prosperity and progress and was ready at any moment to attack them. They are so convinced, especially the young enthusiasts, of the superiority of their way of life, that they take on an air of complacency and of pity for the outside peoples which is found very irritating to some British observers.

But the Russians leave no doubt of their determination to fight with every weapon that science and the devil can devise between them, in case Russia should be attacked by Japan or Germany or any people. They contend that wars are made primarily, almost exclusively, for economic advantage. They will be reassured by the recent news from Japan and China. The government of Nanking is prosecuting an association for armed resistance to Japanese aggression which was established by the widow of Sun Yat Sen, the great leader of the Chinese revolution. The Nanking government is entering into negotiations with the Japanese for joint action for the destruction of the so-called Communists in China. Chiang Kai Shek and his rich merchant supporters would far rather massacre Chinese Communists than Japanese soldiers. "Ha, Ha," Moscow will say. "Didn't we tell you so? Wars are fought for the maintenance of wealth and privilege, not for national independence." And when Chiang Kai Shek sends his band of terrorists to arrest two Chinese generals who had had the temerity to fight against Japanese forces, and when he has those two generals promptly executed, Moscow chortles and queries: "Don't you bourgeois Americans yet comprehend that the struggle between China and Japan is not a struggle between nationalities? It is a struggle between the bourgeois exploiting classes in the two countries against the oppressed, robbed, ravished peasantry and proletariat in both of them?"

Under these circumstances what shall be the national policy of the United State towards Russia? We have recognized Russia. It is not our business as a government to pass judgment upon the domestic organization in any country. We have had diplomatic dealings before with countries whose behavior at home we, the citizens of the United States, would wholeheartedly condemn. The Soviet government is practicing a colossal experiment. Some of its features are good, good beyond peradventure; other of its features are bad, indubitably bad. But it is not for the United States Government to pass judgment; and we have entered into diplomatic relations with them. The economic effect has not been as pronounced as some enthusiasts foretold. Some thought that immediately a great trade would spring up which would relieve the depression at home. Trade has been only slowly stimulated. In March, 1935, the Standard Oil Company made an arrangement to purchase in Russia vast quantities of oil to be distributed by the Standard Oil Company to the different countries of Asia. But few such transactions have gone through.

There was really no reason to expect that recognition of Russia would result in any greater increase of trade than was already growing with countries which had always been recognized. Russia, like the other countries, has failed to meet its debt obligation to the United States. We demand that those debts shall be settled before any governmental aid be given to trade with Russia. Personally I don't see why Russia should be put in any different class from the other nations of the world. If our import and export bank is finding safe business to permit trade with other nations and can find a perfectly safe basis for trade with Russia, so be it. But I should be reluctant to have the government itself drawn directly into these aspects of international affairs.

We don't condemn Russia right off. We don't applaud Russia vociferously. We observe Russia. We examine Russia. We find for the first time in human history a nation trying a completely fresh organization of society, fresh from top to bottom, fresh in all its aspects. We may be sorry for the 160 million guinea pigs who have been subjected to this experiment. We may rejoice with the peasants who during the Tsar's regime were suppressed and oppressed, ravished and robbed, are now lifting their heads for the first time towards the heavens. We can surely rejoice that American ideals are being imitated in the stress upon education, that fruitful, humane experiments in prison administration offset the careless cruelties of the Arctic camps; and we can say in chorus: "May God in his mercy save Russia," though scant parts of its experiment do we care to copy.

CHAPTER VI

Italy

and

Fascism

CHAPTER VI

Italy and Fascism

Fascism is the expression of the personality and experience of Benito Mussolini. To understand Fascism it is essential to understand Mussolini.

When the Great War broke, Mussolini was the editor of the daily Socialist paper *Avanti*, in Milan. That was the climax of his life up to that time. He had previously spent many weary years wandering around Switzerland, Austria, Germany, and Italy, a workman agitator picking up a scant living by odd jobs and writing and lecturing and stump speaking for trade union and Socialist causes. He had been expelled from various countries for his radical, seditious agitations. He had started a little paper of his own, the "Class Struggle."

Two years earlier he had won the exalted position of editor of *Avanti* by criticizing severely the leadership of the Socialist Party and of the labor forces in Italy. The Socialist Party was a strong political party which for thirty years and more had ruled Milan, the city in which *Avanti* was published, had ruled Bologna and various other cities of Italy, and had considerable representation in the House of Deputies.

But Mussolini, two years earlier, had roused the Socialist convention to indignation against the slackness, the fat laziness, the bourgeois luxury of the Socialist and labor leaders, and he had been put into full charge of the Socialist organ, for the purpose of stirring up new indignation in the multitudes and putting new life into the Socialist organization and party activities.

This he had done, sacrificing himself without stint, unwearying in his peregrinations up and down the land. His pen was sharp; his influence became national. He was a revolutionist stirring up the discontented: the agricultural laborers, who in Italy have a different position altogether from the position in the United States, who form a propertyless class existing by day's labor; the industrialists, who, as in the capitalist countries, were wage earners, hired and fired by managers and owners.

When the war broke out, Mussolini quickly demanded intervention on the allied side by Italy. When the German Socialists joined with their war-makers, Mussolini said, "The die is cast. Italy must unite on the side of freedom, the liberation of small nations, the overthrow of Italy's traditional foe and oppressor, the Austrian monarchy."

The Socialist Party, however, was still swayed by the Marxian doctrine that the fundamental struggle is the class struggle within each country, and not the fight between nations. They therefore opposed entrance into the war. They expelled Mussolini from his editorship and from the party. He thereupon started his own organ "The People of Italy," by contributions from his friends, and it was the "People of Italy" (*Populo d'Italia*) that was the oriflamme that Mussolini thereafter waved across his land.

He used this as a fighting organ. The rulers of Italy, the Republicans, were meanwhile dickering for the terms upon which Italy should throw her weight on one side or the other. But the people of Italy, stirred by the appeals against their ancient foes, decided the issue. The London conference settled the terms upon which Italy would enter upon the side of the Allies. *April 1915*

Immediately Mussolini went to the front. He was a fighter by instinct. His love of country amounted almost to an obsession. He was willing to be absorbed by his patriotism, to sink his personality utterly in the State, to give his life freely. When the war was declared his editorial announced, "This day we offer ourselves without reserve or regret; to Motherland Italy we give our lives and our deaths." He was a superpatriot at the front. He fought in the trenches. He was wounded several times. Finally, by the explosion of a trench mortar, his body was riddled with splinters and bullets. In the field hospital he was visited by numerous friends and admirers, for his paper had kept up the fight in the rear. The king called upon him, and his biographer relates that he said to King Emmanuel, "Carry your kind words and sympathies to my comrades who are dying; but, as for me, I must get well and will get well and return to the conflict." He was, however, invalided home and declared unfit for further service.

But he showed anew that the pen is mightier than the sword and with that pen kept the morale of Italian workers, of all those left at home, from decay and disintegration. After Caporetti, the saddest defeat that the Italian army has ever suffered, he blamed the Socialists in part for their defeatist propaganda which had ruined the fighting spirit of the legions, and had enabled the Germans to smash through across the fair plains of Lombardy. He therefore changed the sub-title of his paper from "Socialist Organ" to "The Organ of the Ex-servicemen and Producers" and under that slogan he continued his struggle. I may say that after Caporetti he was seriously sick with nervous prostration and humiliation for seven days, so deeply did he take to heart the struggle, the defeat—temporary, as he declared it must be—of his country.

At the end of the war he found that remnants of the Socialist Party, which was dominated with the idea that the class struggle must be carried forward and that the national struggle was only a fight between hated bourgeois, were stirring up at home antagonism to the returning wounded heroes. When the legions proposed to march through Rome and pass under arches of victory, the government, terrified by these subversive elements, ordered the march to be canceled and the arches to be destroyed. Men in uniform, policemen, officers, soldiers, were insulted on street cars and on the pavements. On one occasion, when officers and soldiers had mounted a train, the train crew refused to move it until the soldiers were expelled. This was an exacerbated anti-patriotism as extreme as Mussolini's patriotism.

The government was supine, cowardly, paralyzed by its own philosophic doubts. Philosophers who were not statesmen but were politicians, were fearful as to whether the doctrine that government is best which governs least would authorize them in going to extreme measures even to execute the police powers of the state. In 1920 a perfect epidemic of strikes afflicted the already suffering body of Italy, suffering with unemployment and destitution, unable to recover its balance after the stupefying blows of the World War. Towards the end of that year peasants were seizing the lands, while workmen seized, took charge and possession of numerous factories in the industrial areas of the north. Some say that Mussolini offered the services of his Fascists to the Socialists who were thus starting revolution. It is to me impossible to believe, considering the history of the last few years between him and the Socialists, that he ever even proffered such a co-operation. Indeed, his critics say that his forces were armed by the imperial army and were loosed on the country to overthrow this incipient revolution. The internal evidence would support the latter hypothesis.

By the next year the movement for seizing the factories had petered out. The government had held its hands, declaring that it was none of its business to interfere in an economic struggle and that, if the strikers and revolutionaries were left to their own devices, they would soon discover the impossibility of operating on a public basis the establishments which they had seized.

Much is made by anti-Fascists of the fact that by 1921, before the march to Rome in 1922, the Bolshevist movement had petered out. Mussolini himself, in July of 1921 in his paper, acknowledged that the strikers had been defeated and their evacuation of the factories effected by their own sense and their experience of the impossibility of their running the factories. On the other hand, in August, 1922, the general strike was declared. Mussolini was then ready to intervene. In 1919 he had been badly defeated when a candidate for the House of Deputies. Thereafter a mob appeared below the windows of his offices yelling, "Down with the bourgeoisie!" "Death to Mussolini! Long live Lenin!" He was undismayed by this demonstration. Pointing to the pistols which he always kept on his writing desk he said, "You need not fear. These people know that I shall get at least two of them before they can get me, and there aren't two among them who dare run the risk."

In 1921 the political tide had turned and he was elected by an overwhelming vote in his own city of Milan. He had called together 150 of his followers and constituted them the Fighting Fascists, the first of the Black Shirts. For two years a civil war, guerilla war, had been in progress. Five thousand Fascists had given their lives in the struggle, and this, to Mussolini, was the greatest demonstration of the power and truth of his doctrine. The turning point had been the assassination by the Socialist municipal government in Bologna of a number of Fascists and Republicans, including one great crippled war veteran, a man whose name was the synonym for valor and sacrifice. That episode stirred the emotions of Italy, and Mussolini became the rallying point for the patriotic and orderly elements who were disgusted with the futility of a government that let guerilla war go on without asserting the State power.

So in 1922 he counted his forces at a convention in Naples —half a million Black Shirts were under arms; fully equipped, regimented, officered by veterans. Other millions—two or three millions—were members of the Fascist Party, and he declared, "We must take over the government as soon as a vacancy occurs." The government itself was shaking, undecided, vacillating; without support, without conviction, without leadership. One strong man knew exactly what he wanted. No strong man sat in an official seat. The prime minister agreed to resign and let the king appoint a new cabinet including the Fascists. After negotiations which lasted only two or three days the king told Mussolini's emissary that the king had refused to sign the order for martial law, and upon Mussolini's insistent demand that he would come to Rome only to make a cabinet of his own, and only upon the written request of the monarch, he entered Rome in triumph at the head of his ordered blackshirted fighting men.

Mussolini became the ruler, more and more absolute as the years have gone on, of his Motherland Italy. His character and his experience are the key to Fascism. Perfervid nationalism, discipline, subordination, sacrifice, the country first, the glory of Italy the supreme goal, Socialism the opposition, the foe; the Socialist Party, a party of traitors; the Socialist doctrines, with which his mind had been impregnated through all his youth and early manhood, to be sifted and tried, only such elements to be accepted and adopted as fitted with this supreme ambition, the exaltation of the country! Mussolini himself says that Fascism is an ordered political philosophy. A doctrine was gradually hammered out in those years of stress and conflict and finally has been brought to finished, polished form. He has written it out, and I hold an authorized translation of his own explanations. Let us summarize it rapidly:

"Fascism is now a completely individual thing, not only as a regime but as a doctrine. Fascism believes neither in the possibility nor the utility of perpetual peace. It thus repudiates the doctrine of Pacifism. War alone brings up to its highest tension all human energy and puts the stamp of nobility upon the peoples who have the courage to meet it."

One wonders why he retains membership in a League of Nations which is pledged to a doctrine precisely opposite. It is like the village soak being an active member of the Total Abstinence Society.

"Thus a doctrine," he continues, "which is founded upon this harmful postulate of peace is hostile to Fascism. And thus hostile to the spirit of Fascism, though accepted for what use they can be in dealing with particular situations, are all the international leagues and societies, which, as history will show, can be scattered to the winds when once strong national feeling is aroused by any motive—sentimental, ideal or practical."

Italy stays in the League only "for what use it can be in dealing with particular situations."

"Fascism repudiates any universal embrace and in order to live worthily in the community of civilized peoples watches its contemporaries with vigilant eyes, takes good note of their state of mind and, in the changing trend of their interests, does not allow itself to be deceived by temporary and fallacious appearances."

This message was surely directed to the address of Adolf Hitler in the Wilhelmnstrasse in Berlin.

Next notice the Fascist social doctrine.

"Such a conception of life," continues Mussolini, "makes Fascism the complete opposite of that doctrine, the base of so-called scientific and Marxian Socialism, the materialist conception of history. Fascism, now and always, believes in holiness and heroism; that is to say, in actions influenced by no economic motive, direct or indirect."

Thus he throws down the gauntlet to Russia and Stalin.

"And if the economic conception of history be denied, it follows that the existence of an unchangeable and unchanging class war is also denied. Above all Fascism denies that class war can be the preponderant force in the transformation of society."

Hardly anything is left, then, of the Socialist doctrine which Mussolini, in his adolescence, gave his days and nights to promulgate. He says nothing about the doctrine of "Surplus Value," which has some relation to the Fascist doctrine of the corporative state.

"After Socialism," he goes on, "Fascism combats the whole complex system of democratic ideology, and repudiates it, whether in its theoretical premises or in its practical application. Fascism denies that the majority, by the simple fact that it is a majority, can direct human society; and it affirms the immutable, beneficial and fruitful inequality of mankind. Democracy is a regime nominally without a king, but it is ruled by many kings—more absolute, tyrannical and ruinous than one sole king, even though a tyrant."—Here peeps out the revolutionary red conviction of his youth.—"Fascism supersedes the antithesis monarchy or republicanism, while democracy still tarries beneath the domination of this idea."

A monarch is a harmless adornment so long as a dictator really rules.

"If democracy may be taken to mean a state of society in which the populace are not reduced to impotence in the State, Fascism may write itself down as 'an organized, centralized and authoritative democracy'."

"The populace not reduced to impotence." That concession is made to the belated falsities of the nineteenth century. He says nothing about his habit of reducing to impotence not only the populace, but the editors, the thinkers, the writers, the leaders, the business organizers, everybody who dares to criticize by thought or word the validity of the doctrines which he has elaborated. With castor oil and castigation he expels everybody who dares to question this Fascism which, like a political pope, he has declared to be the supreme truth. He gives his own version of what is meant by democracy and then repudiates it, his thought always colored by the sad experience of the breakdown of representative institutions in Italy, the feebleness and cowardice and withdrawal from duty of those who had been put in power in Italy in the name of democracy.

Next. "Fascism has taken up an attitude of complete opposition to the doctrines of Liberalism both in the political field and in the field of economics. Liberalism only flourished for half a century. It was born in 1830 in reaction against the Holy Alliance. All the political hopes of the present day are anti-Liberal."

"Fascism has taken up an attitude of complete opposition to the doctrines of Liberalism." By Liberalism he means individualism. He associates private initiative, private ownership of the means of production, free competition, individual striving, along with freedom of the press, freedom against arbitrary arrest, as forming one body of doctrine, and this body of doctrine he repudiates *en masse*.

"All the political hopes of the present day are anti-Liberal." He means that the political hopes of the present day are based upon the control of the economic organization of society. The nineteenth century, he says, was the century of law; the twentieth century shall be the century of labor. The duty of the government is not to reduce its functions to the minimum, but to increase its functions and its power. The doctrines of Bentham and Adam Smith, of the French and of the American political writers of the early nineteenth century, that government must never interfere with business, that it must merely maintain order and keep the ring while in matters material the citizens fight it out between themselves— that doctrine, he says, is fated, bygone. "The twentieth century is the century of collectivism"; therein he retains part of the core of the Socialist doctrine which, in many of its expressions, he repudiates.

"Finally, the foundation of Fascism is the conception of the State." This you will see is the natural outgrowth of his own temperament as expressed during the fighting years. "The Fascist State is itself conscious and has itself a will and personality. Thus it may be called the Ethic State. The State is a spiritual and moral fact in itself. It represents the immanent spirit of the nation." You philosophers will recognize the Hegelian doctrines from which Karl Marx also drew, incomprehensible to the plain man, invoked to rationalize and vindicate opinions and emotions previously adopted. The State above all and before all. Italia, not Deutschland, uber Alles. Liberalism implies individualism, and whoever says Fascism implies the State.

Again. "The Fascist State has drawn into itself even the economic activities of the nation, but leaves a sufficient margin of liberty to the individual. The latter is deprived of all useless and possibly harmful freedom, but retains what is essential."

So the liberal writers and philosophers and malcontents, from Matteotti, who was murdered, down to the forlorn denizens of the Lipari Islands, were "enjoying such freedom as was essential", but they had been deprived of "useless and possibly harmful freedom."

Further ideals of this new style of State challenge twentieth century thought. "The Fascist State is an embodied will to power and government; an ideal of force in action. For Fascism, the growth of empire, the expansion of the nation, is an essential manifestation of vitality, and its opposite a sign of decadence." And "There are a thousand signs which point to Fascism as the characteristic doctrine of our time."

So Switzerland, Denmark, Sweden and other States that have been content within their own boundaries, craving no expansion, aping no bygone empire, have all been decadent. Yet their populations are quite as prosperous and happy and civilized as the people of more pretentious nations. I venture to judge that no countries in the world surpass Denmark and Sweden in the plenitude of life enjoyed by everybody, no nation has fuller or more advantageous control of its government than little, satisfied Switzerland.

Mussolini's own boastful, Gargantuan State ideal is the key to much of his foreign policy. He confuses bigness with greatness.

All Mussolini's philosophic and abstract arguments have been carried on interminably through two or three centuries and will be continued in the future. The fundamental test is not abstract argument but practical operation. The pragmatic test must be applied. In practice what has Mussolini done?

He has asserted the right of the State to control the individual in all his activities. He recognizes that religion has a utility, a validity of its own. He has made terms with the Vatican, relinquishing to the Vatican the purely spiritual training of the young, retaining for himself their control in all their life outside the hours of specific spiritual instruction.

He has cleaned up Italy. The government of Italy had become rotten. The Italian railroads were run with shameful inefficiency. It had been impossible to leave your baggage in the car while you went to the platform or to the restaurant, for thieves would have taken it before you returned. The trains never ran on time. The State railroads shared the crass inefficiency of the political central government. The nation was in conflict, undecided in its mind what to do. The rulers were undecided in their minds, muddled, indeterminate, shilly-shallying; and a strong hand unquestionably benefited the nation in many respects.

But that is no proof of the verity of a denunciation of liberalism and democracy. Capitalist countries ruled by democracies have run their railroads on time and guarded their cars against thieves for decades. Americans have displayed economic and self-discipline power while enjoying civil rights; trains have left New York and reached Miami with marvelous speed and efficiency these many years. Still a citizen may not be arbitrarily arrested, an editor may not be thrown in jail for an article obnoxious to the rulers. You and I may print what we have to say in criticism of Roosevelt and his New Deal. The limitation is set by law. Our actions are controlled by the statutes to which a majority of us in fact as well as in theory have assented.

Cleaning up Italy, while it may be a vindication of a temporary purging in an emergency, is no vindication of the whole body of doctrine which Facism announces. The State, says Mussolini, must be glorified, and any opposition to that purpose must be ruthlessly suppressed. "This explains the necessarily severe measures which must be taken against those who would oppose this spontaneous and inevitable movement in Italy, and would oppose it by recalling the outworn ideology of the nineteenth century." Then Salvemini and Nitti and the other harmless refugee scholars in our midst, the thousands who were punished and driven out of the motherland which they also loved and cherished, must be consoled with the thought that their sacrifice is necessary to the exaltation of the Italian State. The State. What is the State?—an abstraction?—a city in the heavens?—a philosopher's dream?—an idealist's hope? No, the State is right here and consists of institutions and of individuals who work those institutions.

What is the State? Mussolini answered a short time ago. A new cabinet was formed. In that cabinet:

Prime Minister, Benito Mussolini
Minister for Foreign Affairs, Benito Mussolini
Minister of the Interior, Benito Mussolini
Minister of Corporations, Benito Mussolini
Minister of Colonies, Benito Mussolini
Minister of War, Benito Mussolini
Minister of the Navy, Benito Mussolini
Minister of Aviation, Benito Mussolini

The other six offices were distributed among the five and a half million members of the Italian Fascist Party. But, presumably, the "multitude was not reduced to complete impotence."

In practice Mussolini's greatest creation, which he himself says is his greatest contribution to history, is the Corporative State, as it is clumsily called. "Guild State" perhaps would explain it better. Under this conception all production in the country is brought under governmental control and regulation. Every industry and every service is placed in associations. All employers are put in employers' associations, all workmen into labor unions. These are organized first in the communes, next in the counties or provinces, and culminate finally in the national association of employers and the national committee of trade unions. But the trade unions are neither company unions nor a federation of independent labor unions. They are government unions. Their officers are not chosen by the members. They have no walking delegates. Their officers are selected for them by the government. The same with the employers' associations. Their officers are government-appointed and must always be members of the Italian Fascist Party, for loyalty to Fascist doctrine is the first test of political efficiency and fitness. The country is divided into twenty-two corporations. Everything done in the country to produce goods or services is placed in one or the other of these twenty-two categories. These twenty-two head up to the national organizations of each one, and that national organization of each one, including both employers and workmen, appoints delegates to the central committee of corporations. The president of the official committee in each of the twenty-two; the president of the joint corporative committee; the president of the ministry of corporations, which is superior to all of them; the president of every one of them is—who do you think?—the Pooh-Bah, Benito Mussolini. And so Fascism is Mussolini transmuted as the State.

He has insisted on a balance of well-being. He has not sacrificed the well-being of the workman to the profits of the employer. Italy, like all countries, has passed through deep, direful depression. It has been faced with the same insoluble problems as capitalist and socialist countries. It has met them in about the same way. It has established great public works for the relief of the unemployed. It has shortened hours of labor. It has insisted on the distribution of work among a larger number of people. It has withdrawn women from industry to make way for men. It has withdrawn boys under twenty-one to make way for heads of families. It has established unemployment relief. It has shown a consciousness of the needs of the populace. Mussolini's old-time Socialist sentiments have broken through again and again. He is regimenting the nation with almost Stalin vigor. He cannot be accused of establishing an Italy of the rich, nor of serving the interests of property at the expense of the interests of penury. Italy has been consolidated. It has erected an economic social structure which is unique, from which other countries may borrow some features; although I doubt the truth of his prophecy that it will become the dominant system in the civilized world.

I have reserved till last the fatal flaw. Dictatorships and nationalisms throughout history have developed into military tyrannies. Mussolini is fast on the road that brought Napoleon ultimately to ruin. Mussolini exalts force. "War is the supreme expression of the national life", he says. And he has proceeded to militarize the mind of the Italian people to the exclusion of other sentiments. A few weeks ago (January,

1935) he announced the formation of the Ballila, an organization of boys from six to eight years of age, to be read stories of military heroes, to be impregnated with the false heroism of militarism. Children of six taught inhuman barbarities! The flexible minds of the six-year-olds to be distorted to the discredited ideals of Moloch and of Mars! From eight to fourteen they are to be further trained by direct association with those heroes of the nation, the soldiers in barracks. From fourteen to eighteen their spirits are to be subordinated to military purpose—they are to be trained in athletics, so that they may be strong, not to serve, but to fight. Later they will do their year's full service with the army and then, up to thirty-three, they are to be kept in reserve, always at the call of that State which is Mussolini.

Thus his great constructive work in forming the Guild State is surely threatened with ultimate extinction. He sets himself in hostility to his neighbors. He demands, as the Kaiser demanded in Germany before the war, an ever-enlarging place in the sun. Thus far he has won out to considerable degree. Have you noticed that in those peregrinations around Europe by its statesmen, from Poland to Paris and London and Rome and Bucharest and Budapest and Vienna, Mussolini has stayed at home? The mountain will never go to Mohammed. Mohammed must always go to the mountain. The proud rulers of the British Empire have flown repeatedly down to Mussolini, who asserts his personal dignity and the might of his country by insisting that they shall come to him. He will never go to them. Mussolini has compelled France ultimately to yield to him territory in Africa. The agreements of the last weeks culminate a struggle for the expansion of Italy in Africa which has been proceeding under cover for a decade. Italy is to take over a key position on the strait of Bab-el-Mandeb and a large area in the south of Libya.

He can tell his people, perhaps, that his doctrine that a nation is judged by its military strength is, in these respects, working out. The first steps may be easy; so is the descent to hell. But at the bottom of this steep path which he is traversing, at the end of the worship of war, of the glorification of bloodshed, of the idealized enthusiasm for sacrificing peasants to Mars, lies a deep pool of blood which, according to the teachings of all history, unless his course be changed, must finally submerge Mussolini and his suffering nation in red ruin and death.

CHAPTER VII

Germany

and

National

Socialism

CHAPTER VII

Germany and National Socialism

JANUARY the thirtieth, 1935, was the second anniversary of the accession to power of Adolf Hitler, Chancellor of Germany. On that occasion he sent broadcast a speech in which he said:

"The National Socialist regime has lifted up a nation that has wasted away in desperation, and has filled it with strong faith and confidence in the innate and creative powers of its own life, and this is National Socialism's greatest and most decisive aim. The transformation of external symbols has been followed by the transformation of the people's soul. If, on January 30, 1933, I demanded four years' time for the execution of the first Labor Program, then two-thirds of this promise has already been fulfilled in half this period."

Looking back to that date two years ago, we find that no specific promises were made, but three promises were, in general terms, enunciated: (1) The farmer must be relieved from impoverishment. (2) Unemployment must be definitely overcome. (3) Conditions must be established for prosperity in every branch of business. And on Labor Day of that year, reinforcing the expectation of a psychological change, the Chancellor said:

"We want to imbue, nay, burn into the minds of our people: 'German People, you are not a second-class people, even if a thousand times the world wants to have it that way. You are not inferior in value, nor secondary in importance'!"

We will take up in order those four items and briefly survey their accomplishment. We will then pass to a consideration of some of the fundamental articles of the State credo of National Socialism, and finally touch upon the applications of that credo in foreign policy.

131

It may be admitted without question that the psychological change has been effected. Germany has become a self-confident people. The disintegration of spirit which had marked previous years has been stopped. The whole people in face of the outside world has united as one man, determined, self-confident, resolute, even aggressive. This was emphasized anew in the result of the Saar plebicite, which, by an overwhelming majority, demonstrated the desire of the Saarlanders to renew their national allegiance, to enter into the Hitler jurisdiction. The Chancellor is justified in saying that he has transformed the national spirit from a low, debased level of fear, of disintegration. It has been raised, as against the outside world, to a level of confidence, of stern determination as to its own national destiny.

Internally the consolidation, while truly remarkable, has not been so conclusive. Differences of party sentiment as to who shall control this consolidated nation have occasionally been revealed. All Germany, practically, is convinced of the necessity and advantage of being fused into one unbreakable people. But there is not union as to which section or group shall command this elevated allegiance. This breakage, temporary, perhaps, but significant, was shown in the events of June 30, 1934.

Hitler, Goebbels, and Goering, the three most important of the dictators, suppressed with violence, lawlessness, bloodshed, what they termed a conspiracy. Roehm, the commander of the two million Brown Shirts, who had previously been a man of power, whose word carried decisive weight; Ernst, the Berlin commander of the Brown Shirts; and seventy others, by acknowledgment of Hitler himself, (two hundred others, by subsequent revelations), were summarily executed. Most important and startling of the victims were ex-Chancellor von Schleicher and his wife, who, if not tortured, as is claimed by some, was certainly tormented before she was finally killed. This evidence of disruption within the controlling party was never satisfactorily explained, even to the German people, and the world has wondered since: "Will the events actually behind these occurrences remain hidden?" The most erudite German historian of the Nazi Party said that the most likely explanation was that these victims had been carrying on a whispering campaign against the administration throughout Germany, exposing the feet of clay of many of the national deities. That seemed to me to be too abstract and vague an explanation to be satisfactory. But recently the Princess Catherine von Radziwill has made a fuller explanation which appears to piece together the key bits of this picture puzzle.

She says that we must go back to the burning of the Reichstag building for the source of this purging. You remember that just before the final events which determined the supremacy of Adolf Hitler, the Reichstag building was burned. The Communists were accused of being the incendiaries. A trial was held, of long duration. A simple, stupid, Dutchman was found guilty of having set the fire and was executed. Many charges were made that the Nazi Party itself had plotted and executed the burning, but no conclusive evidence to that effect was adduced. The Princess von Radziwill asserts that Roehm had been previously instructed to arrange the burning, that she knows from conversations with the chief plotters at the time, among whom she has moved familiarly, that Roehm insisted, before he would execute the order, that it be given to him in writing and signed. This was done, but before the execution of the order it was rescinded, and he was ordered to restore the original document. He refused to go to Berlin upon Hitler's order and hand back the incriminating paper. Ever since he had been under suspicion. He made, therefore, photostatic copies of the order, which were given to von Schleicher and other important persons. Before the purge of June thirtieth there was a plot for the overthrow of Hitler. According to this plot, the General Staff of the Reichswehr, the army, was to be captured in Berlin, and Hitler was to be finally done away with.

This plot had been the outcome of a series of events beginning with the support of Hitler in his earlier days by a group of rich and titled women, including the widow of the ex-Kaiser, Frau Wagner, and a number of others. These women had secured the support of the Monarchists for Hitler, on the expectation that he could be used as a tool, and then monarchy restored. Later they had procured the financial assistance of the industrial lords of the Ruhr, who also expected to use the demagogue, as they styled him, for their own purposes. Hitler repudiated them both. As one of the industrialists said: "Hitler refused to receive orders." His removal was therefore designed.

But some of the ladies talked, and word got to Hitler and Goebbels and Goering of this incipient insurrection. The results were as I have told. The main purpose in the mind of the soldiers acting under Hitler's orders on June thirtieth was to obtain possession of that incriminating paper which had been given to Roehm. Von Schleicher was involved in the conspiracy, although he had refused to be active with Roehm, whom he distrusted. A color of truth to this interpretation of events is given by subsequent happenings. The highly placed persons in Germany were especially enraged by the assassination of von Schleicher, who was the best military mind in Germany, in addition to having been Chancellor, and of his innocent wife. In December, 1934, almost six months after these events, a great secret meeting was held in the Metropolitan Opera House of Berlin. It was packed with all the notables, civil and military, of the nation. No reporters were admitted. No account of its proceedings was given out. But those whose business it was to pry into such affairs for journalistic purposes declare that the main purpose had been to reconcile the army leaders with the civil power. To do that it had been necessary formally to clear the character of von Schleicher. Treason charged against one of their great leaders was insufferable to the military mind; and von Schleicher's memory was at that meeting cleaned of the pollution. Further, to propitiate the army leaders, as was openly announced later, it was decided that the Brown Shirt troops, formerly commanded by Roehm, should be permanently dis-

banded; the army should be in future the sole safeguard of
Germany, unhindered by the semi-militarized troops who had
been so conspicuous in the life of the nation for two years. In
consonance with that decision the news came a little later that
the Black Shirts, Hitler's special guard, his trusted followers,
his pretorian guards, are also to be reduced: from two hundred thousand they are being brought down to twenty thousand, and these twenty thousand are to be put under the control of the military staff. Of these only two thousand will be
specially armed and specially charged with the protection of
the person of the Chancellor, the *Fuhrer*.

Reports come from Germany about considerable dissatisfaction with the regime. I don't vouch for the truth of the
reports. It is impossible, since there are no official utterances
on the subject, to speak with full authority; but English newspapers have published accounts showing that Communists are
again organizing underground, while Monarchists are determined to restore the *ancien regime*; and Princess von Radziwill ventures the prediction that Hitler's rule will be overthrown by a civil war which will be fomented ere long. However, Hitler's defiant announcement of conscription on the
sixteenth of March and his wholehearted exaltation of the
Reichswehr seem to make his power unshakable.

So much for the consolidation of the nation. Now as to
the three economic aims: "The farmer must be relieved from
impoverishment." The farmer's lot has been considerably improved. He has been the pet of the administration. His prices
have been fixed on a high level, so that the index of food
prices in German cities, compared with the prices in foreign
cities, is 264. More than two and one-half times the world
prices was being paid by the city dwellers of Germany for the
reinstatement among the farmers of previous prosperity. The
farmers have been aided by cheap labor. School children who
are unable to get a job are required to go into the country
and work on the land for their keep. Cooperative associations
for the sale of farm products have been created. The farmer
must hand over a certain proportion of his crops to these co-

operative associations, who then undertake to distribute them for him and bring him a good price. The farmer, even of the peasant order, has been raised to a kind of nobility.

Much farming, perhaps the majority of the farming in Germany, is done on large estates, the landowners being the agricultural Junkers. The peasant owners have been required to maintain family possession of their farms and to hand them on undiminished to their male heirs, in order that the life of Germany may be based on a peasant ownership party rooted in the soil. The farmer has been relieved to a considerable degree from impoverishment.

"Unemployment must be definitely overcome." When Hitler came to power six million were unemployed. In January, 1935, the figure was 2,973,000. It had been down in earlier months much closer to two millions. Unemployment has been abated in the two years, if not definitely overcome. This has been achieved by various methods known to other countries. Great relief works have been started. Great credits have been granted to industrialists to increase their output. The industrialists have been required to distribute their work among larger numbers of workmen. Men under twenty-five have been dismissed from factories and put instead upon labor relief works up and down the country. Women have been taken out of the factories altogether to make places for men. "The woman's place is the home, her function the breeding of future Germans."

Labor camps have been established with notable success, with an efficiency and honesty altogether admirable. They resemble our CCC camps, the part of the New Deal which has met with almost no criticism. Every young man in Germany is required to put in at least six months in one of these camps. Camp workmen are engaged in reclamation work of all kinds, in building roads and draining marshes, in filling up swamps, and in increasing the land available for cultivation that Germany may be made self-feeding. They are trained with a touch of military discipline. They learn to handle their shovels with the precision with which a veteran handles a rifle. At the last Nurnberg convention, no sight was more thrilling than that of 50,000 of these camp boys marching in parade, handling their gleaming shovels with the precision of a well-trained chorus, and exalting the place of the shovel with the sword in the maintenance of the national life.

"Conditions must be established for prosperity in other branches of business." There has been a boom in the last year in German industry. The credits granted to the industrialists, the made work which has been proceeding, and, above all, the rearmament which has gone on apace, making great demands on heavy industry, have all stimulated business so that the industrialists announce, von Krupp for instance, that for the first time they are now in the black, after seven years of red tribulation. Let it be noted, to von Krupp's credit, that he refrained from announcing any dividend, but gave bonuses to his wage-earners and office force.

All this has been accompanied by a real regard for the poor, a determined effort to alleviate their sufferings. "No German shall starve or freeze this winter", shouted the Chancellor, echoing the statement of our own great president: "No American shall starve or freeze." The methods adopted have been different. Each month during the winter in Germany there is a Sunday on which no citizen before five o'clock may eat a meal with any dish costing more than about ten cents. The balance that he would spend for food must be contributed to the National Welfare Relief Fund. At the beginning of the winter the noblest of the land go out with tin boxes and make collections everywhere for this fund. The highest ministers, the greatest generals, all join in this national effort of raising money for relief. The result is a large sum which has enabled the Leader to guarantee that no destitute person shall be left uncared-for, to starve or freeze in silence. It is hard to overestimate the effect of such sympathetic thought upon the allegiance, the emotional adoration of the German people for their leader.

Now what price has been paid for this assuagement of German afflictions? The workmen have been robbed—well, I don't want to use any violent terms,—put it this way: the trade unions have all been dissolved; their funds and properties, which were large, have been confiscated. The employers' associations have recently been given a final thirty days notice to dissolve and become, along with the trade unions, a part of the Labor Front, a State body analagous in some respects to the corporative bodies in Italy. But the employers have saved their funds from confiscation. Everybody in Germany has sacrificed the fundamental civil liberties. No life is guaranteed protection under the law. Arbitrary arrest is regularly practiced; trial in secret by the police tribunal is the regular course. Conviction outside the law, incarceration in penal camps, even death may be inflicted. The court has declared that precedents established by the Supreme Court of pre-Hitler days may no longer be accepted, because then justice was administered with the rights of the accused as the central factor. Now the rights of the State and its protection must be the dominating consideration. That is not just hearsay. That is official pronouncement. Nobody may print or speak in criticism of the government and its actions. Newspapers are all under the closest censorship. As Minister of Propaganda and Public Enlightenment, Dr. Joseph Goebbels controls the output of the radio, the movies, the printing press, and all other means of public education and enlightenment. The institutions of Germany have been transformed. As one liberal of former days said, in discussing the Sedition Bill in Berlin in January: "Oh, we have no longer any interest in civil liberties. They are of a period so long past as to be forgotten. We no longer even discuss them!" This deprivation of civil liberty, destruction of parliament, assumption of complete power by a dictator and his myrmidons, are in accordance with certain fundamental State principles which have been announced. The totalitarian State we have become acquainted with in previous lectures. This is the all-inclusive State endorsed and insisted upon in Germany today.

In one fundamental respect Germany is unique among totalitarian States. Stalin undertook to destroy religious sentiment and conviction. Mussolini made terms with the Vatican and religious life. Hitler has attempted, while leaving the Church intact, to put it under complete State authority and control. He has here met his first signal defeat. He ordered, or his party ordered, that the Protestant churches should submit in the matters of Church government to the authority of Reichsbishop Ludwig Mueller, who had been named by the Nazi Party, and also to permit a pagan religion, the revival of the German mythological religion, to have place in the ecclesiastical edifice. The Protestant ministers rebelled. For eighteen months that rebellion has gone forward, and finally, early in 1935, their victory for a time seemed assured. The Bishop of the Protestant church of Bavaria and of the Protestant church of Wurtemberg had been dethroned by order of Dr. Jager, the lay counsellor of the chief bishop. They refused to accept the orders. They were shut up in their own houses, which were raided by forces of plainclothes detectives. The Bishop of Bavaria attempted to address a great crowd of Protestants who gathered in the plaza outside his windows. He was pulled back by Nazi officials. Thereupon the great mass, thousands in number, marched to the Brown House, the headquarters of the Nazi faith. There they spat upon the ground in contempt for Mueller and clerical dictation. And for the first time since the Thirty Years War there was raised in the air of that Catholic city the solemn strains of the battle hymn of the reformation, "A Mighty Fortress is our God." Before such fervent conviction the stiffest-necked official had to bow. Dr. Jager was dismissed from office, and now the embattled ministers are demanding that their synod be recognized as the legal authority for the Protestant church.

When Hitler had made his peace with the army and consolidated his power the persecution of the Church was renewed, and the authority of the hated Reichsbishop Mueller was strengthened. In April, 1935, church bells in hundreds of Protestant communities were mute on Sunday in protest against the arrest of pastors in Hessen and Saxony. Clergymen were taken into "protective custody" and some were sent to concentration camps. Prayers of intercession for arrested pastors were offered in numerous services, though pastors offering such prayers were themselves liable to arrest and incarceration.

The Confessional (opposition) Synod resolved to make itself finally independent of the State, to separate Church and State completely. The synod addressed a solemn inquiry to the government asking whether it "countenances people being led into the temptation to rise up against God, the Lord of Lords."

Herr Terboven, Governor of Rhine Province, signed a decree threatening fines and jail terms to any one who "under guise of defending religious or dogmatic principles, contravenes and speaks derogatively of any principles of the Nazi movement." Both Catholic and Protestant confessional circles fear that this decree means that any assertion from the pulpit that there are higher values than race, blood or soil will be followed by fines and imprisonment. At such risk will any pastor preach that purity of heart is better than purity of blood, the Most High more to be revered than the German race.

The Catholic church has also fought against absorption by the State. On Sunday, February tenth, Cardinal Faulhaber preached a sermon before a great congregation in which sat the Papal Nuncio as a sign of official sanction, in which he declared, "Any officer who interferes with the confessional schools is subject to excommunication." The Vatican thus far, as in the days of Bismarck, is valorously resisting the domination of the German State.

Even more important in State doctrine than the totalitarian State is an amazing article of faith which probably many of you have heard little about—the Nordic myth, which to fervent Hitlerites is a very evangel of redemption. This myth may be summed up in the words of Dr. Hugo Franck, the Hitlerite Minister of Justice, the highest judicial personage, who, in addressing a national gathering of jurists, judges, and lawyers, and counsellors from all parts of the nation, said:

"We are of opinion that the blood substance of the Germanic race constitutes so permanent and unique an asset of the world as a whole, that we should be justified in counting it the duty of the entire human race in gratitude to safeguard this basic German element, for we know that from this racial substance have issued the highest achievements of man."

What startling self-assurance! Surely there is no sign of self-abasement or self-pity or of second-class power about that vainglorious declaration.

The Ministry of Justice made recently a memorandum which was issued as a basis for a new penal code. In that it was stated:

"The first condition for the new legal order must be that henceforth no Jews, Negroes, or other colored people can be absorbed into the German blood; and further, prohibition of blood-mingling must be so interpreted that mingling is forbidden with members of foreign blood communities."

It is not clear, and I don't assert, that English and American individuals would be legally forbidden in Germany to marry and propagate with one of the transmitters of this holy blood stream, though the words literally mean such arrogant exclusiveness. This doctrine has a popularity and force which cannot be ignored. Time forbids to state its origin and history. It was enunciated most emphatically by Houston Stewart Chamberlin in his "Foundations of the Nineteenth Century," a book which he issued in the last year of that century. It says, in brief, that the Aryan races entered Europe from Asia, that there were three branches, the Kelts, the Slavs, and the Germans, that these three came together in the center of Europe and formed the perfect blend of blood which is now rushing through the veins of all true Germans. A vast mass of erudition was lavished on this flattering, far-fetched hypothesis.

The only evidence in rebuttal which need be mentioned is that of Professor Gordon Rand of the University of Edinboro, acknowledged to be one of the highest authorities on anthropology and archæology. He says: "There is not a trace of Aryan elements in any sense among the first exemplars of civilized life. Aryan originally was a linguistic term and denoted the speakers of a certain group of languages. To speak of an Aryan race is as absurd as to speak of a broad-skulled dictionary." It is as if a future historian should exalt the blood of the Negroes in the United States, and claim that because they were among the great English-speaking peoples of the nineteenth century, they transmitted in purity the civilization and ideals of Anglo-Saxon peoples to posterity.

Most important in practical politics is that this doctrine of the natural overlordship of the Teuton in history, decreed by blood and race, is the reason in Germany today for the persecution of the Jews. Hitler came by his anti-Semitic bias in early days in Vienna, when the atmosphere was overheated with political controversy on the treatment of the Jews. At the beginning of his reign in Germany his doctrine offended many of his followers, but he forced it upon them. The ground of the objection to the Jew, however, is not religious, as it has hitherto been in other lands. The ground is mainly racial. The Jew who becomes a Christian in religious faith and practice is no more acceptable than a ringletted eastern or Galician Jew in kaftan. The same Minister of Justice says:

"Anti-Semites we are and have been from the beginning. We are so, however, not out of hatred for the Jew, but out of love for the German people."

Therefore it is enacted that any person whose grandfather or grandmother had any Jewish blood, racial blood, in their veins, cannot hold office or power, or even exercise the rights of citizenship in Germany. In the two years under review 60,000 German Jews and 20,000 foreign Jews have been either exiled or have fled from Germany. Four thousand doctors and four thousand lawyers have been deprived of their livelihood. Artists, musicians, theatre folk of all kinds, writers, and painters and sculptors, if their bodies were tainted with this alien blood, have been denied the rights which the Kaiser and his predecessors had freely granted; because, says the German State, purity of blood is the prime consideration.

"The Teuton is entitled to, and will attain, by virtue of his race, the overlordship of all mankind. To this grand destiny the German people must look. You are not downtrodden; you are exalted. You are the chosen people of God, and with this former self-declared chosen people, you can have no dealings or commerce. That would be to betray your basic powers and fundamental destiny."

The State credo, then, of Hitlerism, may be summed up: Man is not created equal, but Teutons are created by God superior. Man is not entitled to liberty, but the Teutons are entitled to liberty against all foreigners. Men are not entitled to life except as life is defined by their rulers. The pursuit of happiness is not for the true Teuton, but only the performance of duty, duty defined by his chosen *Fuhrer* or Leader. "Thy people are everything; you individually are nothing" is the motto hung around the walls of the Labor Camps. "We were born to die for Germany" is the doctrine put before their eyes every day. The individual is only an instrument for the creation of the State. And the State with German blood is the most exalted in the world.

You can see that leaders imbued sincerely, deeply, unquestioningly, with such fanatical ideas will try to put them into effect in foreign policies. Therefore, at different times they have announced that they will absorb into the true kingdom all the Teutons now suffering in bondage under the jurisdiction of Czechoslovakia, Russia, Switzerland, Austria. They do not propose immediately to attempt that by war; but they did start a Brown International, competing with the Red Interantional and utilizing its methods. In Austria, at the beginning of last year, there was intolerable ferment caused by Nazis, subsidized and helped in every way from Germany, who demanded that Nazism be made the credo of Austria, in preparation for the economic and political amalgamation with Germany. Chancellor Dollfuss, the petty dictator of Austria, was assassinated in June, 1934, by Nazi emissaries. Thirty thousand had been rallied in Germany from Austria ready to take part in the final fight. Only early in the next year were those forces disbanded. That movement has been checked by circumstances. Hitler declares fervidly that his one desire now is for peace. We will not produce any of the evidence that is advanced to indicate that his cry is only a pretense. We will only say that, accepting his asseveration, he is now being put to the test by the nations of Europe. His policies have welded into one, all the nations of Europe except Poland, against Germany. He did a signal service to Europe and mankind by healing the deep, painful wound of the Polish Corridor. With Poland his relations are peaceful. The rest of Europe, including England, has become deeply suspicious. In February, 1935, he was offered treaties of peace and amity with guarantees for their performance by England, France, Belgium, Italy, Jugoslavia, the Baltic States, and Russia.

Hitler in his mountain home in south Bavaria, surrounded by his advisors, considered his answer. After making an evasive verbal reply he finally repudiated all legal restraints and announced on the sixteenth of March that Germany would in future ignore the Treaty of Versailles and create an army, by conscription, over half a million strong, trained and equipped to the highest pitch of efficiency. Later negotiations showed that the German air power was already equal to Britain's, and that Hitler means to build a navy of 400,000 tons and to demand the return of German colonies as a condition for returning within the fold of the League of Nations. His armed man power in reserve will increase each year by 350,000. Will his arrogance increase in proportion? That is Europe's riddle.

To Sir John Simon, Foreign Minister, and Sir Anthony Eden, Lord Privy Seal, Chancellor Hitler offered, somewhat impudently, a firm alliance against France. He was told that they had come to make new friends, not to betray old friends.

Hitler's attitude has alienated Mussolini, a cold realist in affairs international. When dictators disagree, who shall decide? Mussolini says that war is inevitable unless either Hitler reduces his claims or Britain joins the continental powers in ringing Germany with bayonets. Believing, like Hitler, that a nation's influence in international councils is proportionate to its armed strength, Mussolini, in April, called to the colors large reinforcements. At the Stresa conference on the eleventh of April he spoke in the tones of the master of legions.

Russia regards Germany and Fascism as the enemy of Europe as Hitler regards Russia and Communism as the enemy of civilization. Russia received the British envoy most cordially. Stalin himself by his deep knowledge of European politics and his calm and restrained manner, favorably impressed the phlegmatic English aristocrat. Russia seeks British assurance of aid against German aggression, specifically against a German and Polish raid on the Ukraine. Russia and Poland were made the more apprehensive by the Nazi tactics in April in Dantzig, the city given by treaty to the control of the League of Nations, where the German Nazis repeated the election tactics which they had developed in the Saar, though their onslaught failed to win the two-thirds majority requisite to convert Dantzig into a totalitarian State on the Hitler model. But Poland, lying between Germany and Russia, and likely to be the battle ground if these two go to war, is reluctant to join in any pact with either against the other.

Britain will probably seek, tirelessly, for some means of winning joint security through cooperation based on the League of Nations. If France and Italy and Russia could place reliance on Germany's signature perhaps Britain could succeed. Though, even then, Germany's habit of demanding more after each concession would make Britain's search like following a mirage. Paradoxically enough, the deep yearning for peace that fills the hearts of the British people, makes the task of the government in one respect the harder. In proportion as Hitler is convinced that Britain will neither fight nor make a Continental alliance, his self-assurance is likely to grow. While the threat of his air fleet stirs Britain, the Labor party is so determined against war that an alliance against Germany would become an election issue. Only the most flagrant repudiation by Germany of all conciliatory approaches can unite Britain in favor of a plan of encirclement.

Yet war in the near future is unlikely. This is the judgment of two of the world's most competent observers, Edouard Benes, Foreign Minister of Czechoslovakia, and Anthony Eden, Lord Privy Seal. All the peoples are agonizingly against war. Except possibly the Germans. And Germany will not be ready for war for several years. An army cannot be equipped to the last button and trained to the last tactic in a few months. Nor can a navy be built over night. France, Italy and Russia will hardly start a preventive war, though the existing alignment in Europe would make the destruction of Germany almost certain. Not enough is at stake to risk so dreadful an expedient; though war may ultimately burst, for, as Stanley Baldwin, President of the Council, said: "I am not a pessimist, but I see the nations walking the road that leads to war."

Britain will hope to keep postponing an outbreak, always in the expectation that either Hitler will be displaced by a less bellicose ruler, or that Germany's economic troubles will bring him to terms or that the German nation will be appeased by possessing an army and will not risk using it. Germany has not alleged that its disarmed condition has caused it any physical loss; but only that its spirit was mortally injured by the military deprivation. Perhaps the nation, absorbed in goose-stepping and air flights, will be cured of its inferiority complex and will sincerely join its neighbors in good relations.

These darkening war clouds, gathering, now east, now west, constantly threatening, never dispelled, fill American citizens with dismay and anger. They make American appeals in favor of unity with the League of Nations fall on stony hearts. Never again! never again! is the exclamation heard everywhere, never will we take any part in Europe's quarrels. We have failed to assuage Europe's internecine bitterness. We will take no sides in Europe's quarrels.

With dictators in autocratic power over vast armies in sev-

eral countries Europe's outlook is dismal. For this is the final
lesson of dictatorships. Dictators bring war.

Our review of dictatorships is concluded. Next we shall
consider the three great peoples who still march under the
banner of democracy, who have not sold their birthright for
a mess of pottage:—France, the country of liberty, equality,
fraternity, that disturbing slogan that was first hurled over
the absolute monarchies of Europe; England, the mother of
nations, whose Union Jack floats on every sea, carrying to
every people the message of law, order, parliament; and our
own well-loved country, the melting pot of the white races,
which has subdued a continent to the plow, and attained unequalled riches and power, inspired by the ennobling sentiment, "Man is endowed with certain inalienable rights, among
which are life, liberty, and the pursuit of happiness."

CHAPTER VIII

The

Democracy

of

France

CHAPTER VIII

The Democracy of France: Liberty, Equality, Fraternity

THE New York *Times* correspondent at Geneva, after wandering backwards and forwards over the United States last autumn on a vacation, reported that France remains the country most misunderstood by Americans. It is therefore not superfluous for us to study the present situation in France, the foundations of its domestic and foreign policies.

France today is baffled by three quandaries which it faces simultaneously: parliamentary instability, economic distress, foreign menace. We will consider these in turn; but, as introduction, note that the French democracy, like the other democracies of the world, is confronted with a problem inescapable, baffling, and yet demanding solution at the cost of national stability and peace: the problem of adjusting the national life to the results of the industrial revolution.

During the nineteenth century political democracy was being established. At the same time a quiet but potent revolution without connection with soldiers or government, a revolution of science and discovery and business organization fateful in its consequences, bringing possible plenty to mankind, but upsetting irrevocably the doctrine which at the beginning of the century held almost universal sway, the doctrine that industry needed nothing for its perfect functioning but to be left alone by government, and that by an automatic process, chiefly expressed in the rule of supply and demand, the well-being of everybody would be secured, if only business were left unmolested by the rude, rough hand of the State. France, the first home of democracy, was disturbed by the arrival of this industrial revolution, although less drastically than England or the United States. France is making a noble, a heroic effort today to adjust its government and economic organization so as to procure actually, everywhere, the greatest good of the greatest number. But France is baffled and distressed, first, by parliamentary instability.

In May, 1932, a general election was held at which a heavy majority was given to the Radical and Socialist parties. It was an election somewhat analagous to the first Roosevelt election in the United States. Within the House of Deputies, however, there is a great diversity of groups which makes the operation of parliamentary government difficult. The House of Deputies, which many of you have seen, has great banks of seats ranging around in a semicircle. The Deputies are seated according to the color of their political complexion, ranging from the extreme right of the Monarchists, who have an academic interest in the restoration of the monarchy, way over through every shade of opinion, Republican Right and Republican Center and Republican Left to the Radicals and the Radical Socialists and the pure Socialists and the Neo-Socialists and the Communist Workers and so on all the way to the extreme left of the avowed Communists. And the government in France must always maneuver to obtain from this spectrum mixture sufficient support to keep it in power.

In May, 1932, there was a combination in the elections of the Radical Socialists, as they are usually called in our newspapers, though they are more properly called Radicals, (they represent in reality the interests of the small business people and small farmers and stand for liberal ideas) with the avowed Socialists, who stood at that time unitedly for a Marxian program analagous to the program of the Russian Communists. However, since then two divisions have occurred. Almost as soon as the House assembled it was found impossible for Herriot, the great learned stout leader of the Radicals, to unite with Leon Blum, the long-time leader of the Socialists. The Socialists demanded more change in governmental policy than the Radicals could offer. Later, considerably, the Socialists themselves split and a new group, called the Neo-So-

cialists, was established, on account of the Fascist Nazi Socialist success in Germany. A number of the Socialists decided
that the class war within the nation was not the all-important
struggle, that the national life must be sustained against aggression in order that the individual life and social reform
might be advanced. The Neo-Socialists broke away from
the old Socialists and adopted a new motto: order, authority, nation. They have become one of the most effective and
strengthening forces in French life.

However, this government of the Radicals and left, the
Cartel des Gauches, immediately got into troubled waters.
France was experiencing, a year or two later than other countries, the business depression. Unemployment increased, bankruptcies multiplied, farmers were dissatisfied, tax collections
fell off, and, despite new taxes, sometimes heroically applied,
the budget could not be balanced. Upon that fundamental
issue one government after another toppled. The Socialists
objected to the method of cutting down Civil Service salaries
and imposing heavy taxes, arguing that other and more modern, Rooseveltian, ways of recovery should be adopted. One
government after another fell, the changes always being accompanied by a re-shuffling of the cabinet positions, never,
however, up to the end of 1933, involving admission of the
right members of the House into governmental power.

Towards the end of 1933 France was in a parlous state
politically. The country was disgusted with the instability of
the government, with its failure to govern. The distress was
deepening. The situation in Germany, with Germany withdrawing from the Disarmament Conference and announcing
its intention to rely on force, to rearm despite all treaties, and
to face France with an accomplished fact, was menacing: all
this taken together caused throughout France a sense of in-
security, a fear of the future, an uncertainty as to its fate in
the next few years.

In the meantime there had been established in France several organizations which grew rapidly in strength and were
in the main anti-parliamentary, although they denied, usually,

that they desired a Fascist regime. Yet on the whole they were semi-Fascist and all of them stoutly anti-Socialist and anti-Communist. With the Socialists they coupled the Radical party under Herriot, which was the dominant party in the House of Deputies.

These organizations were, first, the *Action Francaise,* with 60,000 active members, a purely royalist organization with an organ of tremendous biting ability and a writer, Leon Daudet, whose words were gospel in the castles and in the rich districts of Paris. They had a fighting youth organization, the *Camelots du Roi,* which started the system of going into the streets and demonstrating by a show of force against the government. The Young Patriots, another organization with an able leader and 240,000 members, had an analagous policy. Not at all Royalist, but particularly anti-Communist and anti-government, the *Solidarite Francaise* with 250,000 adherents, was an analagous organization drawn in part from the old soldiers. It was established at enormous cost by the perfume manufacturer Coty, who ruined himself by the money that he lavished upon this organization and upon the newspaper which he established, supplemented by the tremendous costs of an unfortunate divorce suit. The combination of rampant politics and domestic infelicity destroyed even his huge fortune. Then, more important for practical purposes than the others, was the Fiery Cross—*Croix de Feu*—headed by an old soldier of ability and character, Colonel de La Rocque. It was organized on somewhat the same principles as Mussolini's blackshirts, a disciplined group numbering 50,000 as a minimum, with a hundred thousand at least of extra sympathizers in their families, ready at the call of their leader instantly to take to the streets.

Below these were numerous small groups of intellectual and youthful idealists, the *Ordre Nouveaux, Hommes Nouveau, Nouvelles Equipes,* the new this and the new that, a dozen of them, all fervently patriotic, all deeply dissatisfied, all desperately determined. France was a caldron of political discussion, of newspaper agitation, of armed or semi-armed incipient revolt.

The movement culminated February sixth of last year (1934). To stimulate the discontent a financial scandal had broken, the Stavisky scandal. Stavisky was a scoundrel of the first water. Of Russian birth, he had been brought up as a Catholic in France by a respectable dentist father who was ultimately driven to suicide by his son's crimes. Stavisky had first swindled on a small scale and got higher and higher in the disreputable half-world twixt respectability and the underworld, the world of racetrack gamblers, of dope peddlers, of cafe habitues, of small criminals who utilize stronger criminals for their own purposes. Eventually he made a false step in swindling a stock broker of some $70,000. He was indicted but never brought to final trial. Nineteen times his case was adjourned. He entered upon a swindling career, first in connection with the Municipal Pawnshop at Orleans, then at the Municipal Pawnshop at Bayonne. The Municipal Pawnshops in France are semi-governmental. They are managed under strict rules, and are banking institutions of some credit and respectability. Stavisky, by corruption, bribery, the duplicity and complicity of officials, managed to have some emeralds highly overvalued, practically valueless stones estimated at the worth of the rarest jewels, and upon that security issued bonds. As the time came for taking up his indebtedness, he attempted a fraud on a still larger scale, buying up worthless Hungarian bonds which, with the aid of his political connections, he hoped to see accepted by the Security Fund of France as part of its assets. He was exposed, and fled. The pursuit was slow and incompetent, and finally, when the detectives surrounded the house in which he had taken refuge, a shot put an end by suicide to his miserable life.

France was deeply stirred by these revelations, because they indicated that while the taxpayers were sweating blood to pay their government obligations, while hundreds of thousands were unemployed and starving or semi-starving, some government personages were reveling in illicit luxury. Let it be said at once, however, that the number of Deputies concerned with Stavisky either as legal representatives or in more heinous capacities was very limited, relatively, to those involved in other previous scandals; and that the Radical party drummed out of its fold every lawyer who had appeared for the defense of this rascal. But, unfortunately, this exposure added fuel to the fire. *Action Francaise* filled its front pages day after day, and other papers followed suit, with inflammatory articles based on either truths, half-truths, or whole lies, about governmental complicity in this blackguard's frauds and loot. After a government of only two weeks' duration had been overthrown, Deladier consented to try to form a new government, he having served as prime minister a year earlier and having conducted a government of great merit, staunch, stable, and unexcited. The previous government had been overthrown without a majority being registered against it in the House. This was in itself a disturbing precedent. When, on February sixth, it was announced that the new government would meet the House of Deputies, the Fascist and semi-Fascist organizations at once issued a call to arms. The newspapers of February sixth, in hundreds of thousands of copies, called flamboyantly on the people of Paris to bestir themselves: "down with the assassins, down with the murderers, down with the robbers." *Action Francaise* issued a call in great headlines, "against the assassins, against this abject government; everybody, tonight, in front of the Chamber." The Chamber itself met in the afternoon. The prime minister arose to make his statement of ministerial policy. He was howled down by the extreme right of the Royalists and their sympathizers and the extreme left of the bakers' dozen of Communists. For the first time in the history of the Third Republic the session had to be adjourned by the speaker in the midst of a first ministerial declaration. On his return he was allowed to finish amid great uproar, and all through the afternoon and evening the speaking and the shouting continued,—democracy talking itself to death.

Towards half-past six, as the apprehensive Deputies looked

out of their doors across the bridge which they faced over the Seine, they saw crowds assembling in response to the inflammatory appeals that had been issued. The crowd gathered thicker and thicker. The Republican Guards and the police were pitifully insufficient. They barricaded with police vans the two ends of the bridge, so as to prevent the seething crowds in the Place de la Concorde across the river from reaching the House which was their wished-for prey. About seven o'clock an excited member of the Right rushed into the House of Deputies and shrilled, pointing at the Prime Minister: "Shots have been fired. Have you ordered the firing, you assassin?" As the Chamber emptied into the more exciting precincts outside the walls, a scene of mob fury rarely paralleled was noticed. The crowds, sometimes marching in order behind the banners of the *Croix de Feu* and the *Solidarite Francaise* and the *Camelots du Roi* and the rest, converged ever thicker upon the Tuileries and the Place de la Concorde. Finally, according to the testimony subsequently adduced, the defenders were compelled to fire. The rioters, even those who at the beginning were orderly, as they were reinforced with hooligans and the elements from the underworld, always eager for disturbance and loot, became more and more dangerous. The Marine Department was deliberately set on fire by gasoline torches thrown through the windows. At one moment old soldiers, exasperated and excited, charged upon the barricades of police vans, ran along the parapets on each side, and struck down the defenders who were not already wounded or in hospitals, so that only by real bullets fired at human targets could the forces of order prevail. On that night seventeen were killed, 1300 wounded. The battle was not one-sided, for sign boards and asphalt and broken chairs and the balustrades from the whole region were demolished to make weapons for the crowd. The House itself crept out towards nine o'clock through the back door. The streets were barricaded; lights were out; only the glare of a burning bus lighted them on their way. Herriot was seized by the mob which started to carry him to the Seine to throw him into the water. He was rescued by another group that recognized him.

No wonder that next morning all Paris palpitated. Was this the Fascist *coup d'etat* in imitation of Mussolini and Hitler? Was the government, the republic, to be destroyed? Could France recover and reassert its dignity? The governmental crisis continued. At first the prime minister declared he would not resign. But in the course of the day he determined that he could not depend upon the police and that the army might not obey cabinet orders. He determined for the safety of the nation to resign. The eighty-one year old Marshal Lyautey had gone to President Lebrun during the day and, it is credibly stated, had told the president that if the ministry did not resign, he himself would lead veteran forces on Paris. The government did resign, and it was immediately announced that the elder statesman Doumergue would form a cabinet. Then, just as suddenly as the straw fire had flared up, it died down. The street had won its way by the overthrow of the Radical government and the installation of a conservative, elderly man in power, and was persuaded to drop further demonstrations that night.

Two days later a responsive demonstration was arranged by the Communists in the Place de la Republique, a demonstration which was handled much more roughly than the silk-hatted demonstration of the Royalists and Fascists and semi-Fascists. One week later, the trade unions, determined to show that France would not submit to any Fascist *coup d'etat*, ordered a general strike for 24 hours, merely as a demonstration of the solidarity of the working class and their unshakable determination that a parliamentary regime and democracy should live. The general strike was a success, accompanied by no disorder. No newspapers were published; no taxis, no subways ran. In different cities of the country the same demonstration was made. Especially the civil service went out *en masse*, the civil service being in France a very much more inclusive body than here, including for instance all the teachers and professors of the land. So, after these exhibits and counter exhibits of public opinion and public exasperation France speedily quieted down.

Only one other highly disturbing fact occurred, for the Stavisky scandal was still unsolved, unsettled, judicially undetermined. One afternoon the body of the magistrate, M. Albert Prince was found, mutilated, lying across the railroad tracks near Dijon. Was he murdered, or had he committed suicide? Murder by the Stavisky gang with the collusion of the police was the immediate theory of the discontented Right-Wingers and Doumergue's new government was slightly shaken, almost before it had got settled down. However, the abuses and inefficiency and want of coordination in the police department and in the governmental departments were accepted as something to be solved within the parliamentary framework. Considerable inefficiency was revealed. The hostility between the national detective force and the Parisian police force, for example, which made the discovery of criminals incredibly difficult, was almost unbelievable, even to us Americans who are accustomed to police inefficiency. But it was agreed that nothing connected with Stavisky or the murdered magistrate warranted the discarding of parliamentary principles.

Doumergue lasted eight months, a period of convalescence for the nation. He was trusted. His cabinet was a national cabinet, including everybody from the Neo-Socialists on the left, clean across to the Royalists on the right. He was supported out of loyalty. The Socialist leader, Leon Blum, more than once said that he did not approve of this or that measure, but for the sake of preserving the republic he should vote for the government. The antagonism of foreign powers was the overbearing consideration through a great part of the time. But after eight months Doumergue's mission ran out. He viewed the problem as purely political. He called almost exclusively for reforms of political machinery, and the citizens knew and many of the Deputies knew that the problem was mainly economic. When he insisted that the budget should be voted by decree, that the House and the Senate should travel to Versailles and hold a new constitutional convention which would give the president, on the advice of the prime minister, the power to dissolve parliament, as is done in England; when he insisted on drastic cuts in the civil service salaries as the main method of procuring economic recovery, he was finally discarded and went back, like Cincinnatus, to his farm;—honorable, able, patriotic, devoted, but a little *passe*. He was succeeded by the present prime minister, Pierre Etienne Flandin, a man of the Right, a business man with a good war record and with experience of America, and other countries.

Flandin at once changed the tone of the principal proposals. He said: "Our problem is mainly to put the industries of France once more at work, to solve the problem of the farmer and of the grape grower, to bring prosperity to those three quarters of the population who are small business people, small manufacturers, small farmers, small shopkeepers, not members of great cartels or trusts." He surveyed the economic scene, and truly it was distressing, for as France entered upon the depression late, France is recovering late and France today is near the bottom of the trough. Bankruptcies have continued. Unemployment has risen to 450,000, a number insignificant to Uncle Sam but rather portentous, absolutely unparalleled in France. That number includes only the unemployed on the insurance fund, improperly called the dole by critics, and does not include by any means more than a fraction of those who are without work. Flandin immediately proposed measures resembling those with which we have become acquainted. The farmers were in distress; unsold wheat had been accumulated in the barns. The mistaken policy had been adopted earlier, of which we have also heard, of stimulating the price, fixing a high price governmentally without restricting the acreage, with the inevitable result of an increased crop and a stupefying surplus. The same had occurred with respect to the grapes, a standard industry. So the new ministry has arranged to take over these surpluses, disposing of them in various ways, imposing a processing tax to pay the cost, and slowly eliminating the fixed government price.

Further, it is proposed now, and it was endorsed less than a week ago (Feb. 1935) by a huge majority in the House of Deputies, to put French industry under codes, as we would style them. The French industrialists are to be encouraged to organize themselves. They are to be permitted to put restrictions upon production, to impose good behavior upon a recalcitrant minority, to bring order by themselves into the producing machine, all dependent upon two-thirds to three-fourths of members, and the government, through experts and committees, having the final word of approval or disapproval. The prime minister, as far as one can judge, adopts this as his rule of policy: the method of organization shall not be the ownership of the industries by the government, as the Socialists advocate, but on the other hand there shall be some control by the government, in order that the security and liberty of the individual workman and the individual farmer and the individual shopkeeper shall be assured. A mixture of corporatism, as Mussolini has practiced it, a slight infusion of the ideas of the Socialists, a strong determination to sustain the long-cherished ideas of democracy of the whole French nation!

That brings us to the foreign situation, which we must briefly review. Almost all that the average American citizen knows or cares to know about France is that France has refused in the last two years to pay the instalments of the French debt to the United States. That finishes it. But we who want to form judgments based on facts, on history, on rules of equity, must remember that France has a grievance against the United States. This is the way the Frenchman looks at the history of the United States and France since the war. (I speak now not for myself, but for the French.)

President Wilson agreed with France at the peace table that America and England would unite in a treaty of protection for France against German aggression. In return for that agreement Clemenceau and the French leaders accepted the treaty which denied to France the neutrality of the left bank of the Rhine which, had it been assured, would, our military leaders state, have protected us then and protected us today, so that we need have had no worry about Hitler and his bellicosity. When President Wilson returned to the United States the Treaty of Versailles was rejected by an unholy combination of the extreme right, headed by Senator Cabot Lodge, and the extreme left pacificists who announced for all the world to hear that the Versailles Treaty was a *pot pourri* of all wickedness.

That cry they have sustained ever since. America encouraged Germany in the view that Germany was an injured innocent and France a monstrous tyrant, squeezing the life out of new Germany and holding her to a contract of slavery. Every time that concessions were made by France,—through the Dawes Plan and the Young Plan on reparations, for example, agreements which were signed by Germany not under duress, but willingly,—the German demands grew louder and more strenuous. Never was satisfaction expressed for any concession made nor ever any honest attempt made to come to an agreement with the late foe.

Finally, after America had poured, through its private investors, billions of dollars into Germany, President Hoover, without saying to France, "by your leave", demanded a moratorium of all international debts, in the hope that if government debts were canceled, privately-incurred debts would be paid. President Hoover made a sort of seventy-five per cent assurance to Prime Minister Laval, a few months after the moratorium, that if only France would be generous, cancel all reparations, extend a hand of friendship to Germany, receive Germany as a prodigal into the family of nations, then the United States would cancel the debts, world prosperity would be assured and peace would settle like a beneficent dove over Europe. Prime Minister MacDonald also assured the French delegates that he knew the heart of the American people, and that they could confidently rely upon American cancelation, if only they would "take the initiative", — a phrase used in the official communication after the conversations between Laval and Hoover. So reparations were canceled, but did Germany settle down? On the contrary, the strength of Hitler grew after every concession: withdrawal from the Rhine years before the treaty term, first reduction, and finally complete cancelation of reparations,—but Germany always became more intransigeant.

Just before Germany withdrew altogether from the League of Nations and the Disarmament Conference France, accepting the advice of England and America, granted the principle of military equality, but again the concession was answered by more defiant measures.

And now what do we see?—says France. World prosperity has not been restored by any of the measures which were taken and which we were promised would bring restoration. Germany has not been conciliated. The military clique in Germany has been reinstated in its old power and dominance. The Junkers in government in Germany sustain in unbroken vigor their old theories, made even more obnoxious, and so we ask you Americans—say these Frenchmen: "Is the wrong entirely on our part, and is the righteousness entirely on your part? It was easy for you idealists to cherish Germany and demand every reduction of the penalties imposed upon her, but when it came to sacrifices by your own country you proved powerless to get your government to ratify your wishes for cancelation favorable to France."

Hoover may have had that in mind when he issued his moratorium, but the American people have refused to back him, and France is left with the German reparations, on which she relied and which Poincare assured the House of Deputies were a condition for the fulfilment of the Mellon-Beranger agreement, canceled.

German reparations have been canceled and the French debts are still on the books. That is the French case in the matter, a case, I submit, which deserves consideration. At any rate a part of that stream of idealist sympathy which ran so strongly towards Germany for a decade might perhaps now be diverted to sunny France from which for so long it has been held back.

That brings us to the relationship between France and Germany. Hitler embodies, as we have seen, the Junker faith *in excelsis*. France has sought consistently in season and out of season just one thing, national security. Many of us at different times were irritated at French insistence upon that aim. We said for some years, many of us, including myself: "Why can't France trust to the League of Nations? There is a covenant of protection for everybody. Why does France seek a special security?" France has consistently, persistently, insisted that the League of Nations must be accepted as the final arbiter, and that within the framework of the League of Nations any modifications of the Treaty of Versailles must be made. But the League of Nations, as France feared, has proven inadequate as soon as a serious situation arose. To small situations, yes; the League was adequate. But to bring Japan to terms—Japan, the Germany of Asia—the League covenant was too feeble. And so the Frenchman says: "We tried consistently to win security through international agreement. Now we must turn to the alternative method, which we have always had in mind, the isolation of Germany; for remember: Germany is the enemy." In the policy of isolation the recent government has been successful beyond its expectations.

England, on which France always relies primarily for mutual protection, has also come round to recognize that the German air fleet is the menace, the enemy. England is convinced that Germany has rearmed. England has discovered and announced that her frontier is no longer the white cliffs of Dover, but the rushing waters of the Rhine. And so England and France and Belgium and Italy have proffered to Germany a new agreement based on these fundamentals: first, the existing borders of European States can only be changed by united action; only within the terms of the League covenant, and by action of the League of Nations, as contemplated in the Treaty of Versailles, can changes be ratified;

second, these five great powers will spring to each other's defense if one should make aggression; a sudden excursion in the air over the Rhine one way or the other shall be answered instantly with converging fleets of airplanes from the different nations rushing to the defense of the threatened country. On the eastern side an Eastern Locarno is proposed: Russia, Poland, Germany, the Little Entente, agreeing also that their countries are not to be disturbed by any militant aggressor.

The generals of France tell the ministers that they would prefer Hitler should remain in power rather than the German generals replace him, as they are threatening to do; for Hitler, fortunately for France, alienates England. Hitler probably has alienated also most idealists in America. He has done his best within recent weeks to strengthen that alienation by beheading in medieval form and with medieval circumstance two women charged with spying, thus demonstrating anew the inability of the Junker mind to comprehend the effect which acts will have upon the minds of other countries.

Two years of probable peace is accepted by the French as a respite. Imagine it! Imagine our state of mind if we felt there was a practical certainty that in two years we should be involved in a great war, despite all our efforts to prevent it.

I know and you know that France has by no means been blameless through the years since the war. What nation has been blameless? Great Britain? The United States? We are all human beings animated by different purposes; all seeking life, some seeking liberty, all desiring means of happiness.

My concluding word is simply this. France is a distressed people, with all its failings the exponent in Europe of the grand principles of government that have saved the world during the nineteenth century. Shall we in America continue our petty pin-pricking of France? We have ceased slapping so cordially on the back her neighbor Germany. Shall we not also realize that France is a democracy with our ideals, a people struggling valiantly to be free, and towards them shall we not stretch across the Atlantic the warm hand of fellowship?

CHAPTER IX

Democracy

in

Great Britain

CHAPTER IX

Democracy in Great Britain: Law, Order, Parliament

After the Great War, which was fought, we imagined, to make the world safe for democracy, we have been dismayed and stupefied to find democracies all around the world overthrown, and dictatorships, more or less absolute, established: Russia, Jugoslavia, Bulgaria, Austria, Germany, Italy, Portugal, Spain; the majority of the populations of Europe now subject to rule without constitution and without popular approval. In South America hardly a nation has enjoyed, during the last decade, a stable government under a constitution accepted by a majority of the people. We realize that one factor has spread over the whole world to contribute to this debacle of popular government. That factor has been the breakdown of business organization, the collapse of the great structure of credit and debt and currencies and gold systems which had been erected in the nineteenth century over the world.

Yet the veritable center of that system stood like a Gibralter, firm and immovable in its democracy amid the world storm. London was at the center of the web of international finance. No tremor anywhere but had its effect in London. Banks and firms might go under in Singapore, in Hongkong and Buenos Aires, in San Francisco, in New York—anywhere around the globe—and the effect was transmitted along the webs of finance to be felt in Threadneedle Street. Ultimately Threadneedle Street also was humiliated; but in the downfall of the British gold sovereign the forms and control of democracy were preserved. England has faced the criticisms of Fascists and Nazi Socialists and Communists with brave heart, undismayed.

When we speak of democracy, we are including much more than the machinery of representative government. We are thinking also of those fundamental guarantees of life and liberty, without which the free soul would rather die. And in judging England we must recall that there these fundamental liberties were attained earlier than in any other country. It was more than seven centuries ago on the meadows of Runnymeade that the barons first won from a dissolute king those foundation rights, many of which have been so heedlessly renounced in countries of continental Europe. It was said of the monarch John, "Foul as it is, Hell itself is defiled by the fouler presence of John." Arbitrary, cruel, he utilized his high intelligence only to make more unbearable his lawless tyrannies. After some defeats abroad he was brought to terms on that lovely afternoon in 1215 and made to sign a Magna Carta, the great charter, which has remained the very foundation stone of Anglo-Saxon liberties. He then swore that no man should be arrested, imprisoned, prosecuted, except through the agency of the Great Council. And ever since then, growing from precedent to precedent, the people of Anglo-Saxon lineage have enjoyed these securities, almost as unconscious of their blessings as they are unconscious of the vitality of the oxygen in the air they breathe. "Trade follows the flag" has been the saying in Britain these many years, but more important to humanity: "Magna Carta follows the flag." Magna Carta was an invisible, precious freight in the Mayflower and is today the very substructure of the legal system of the American republic. So it would never occur as a possibility to the English citizenry that they could sacrifice these deeply cherished liberties for the promise of making their railroads run on time, for the promise of cleaning up their country, for the promise of giving them heart or hope in facing foreigners.

Next, look at the attitude of Britain towards the machinery of democracy, which has been so widely condemned. Britain says, through the mouth of Lord Reading, "We know no other way. Representative institutions with citizens voting for their rulers we have developed through decades, through centuries, and that is the only way we know to extend the blessings of self-government to new nations." Today in the British parliament is being discussed the India Bill, which arranges for the extension of these representative institutions over that great subcontinent for the government of the 350 millions that inhabit it. Three hundred and fifty millions to be brought under the benign influence of democratic institutions, an offset to the millions on the continent of Europe who have renounced these institutions. This bill is the outcome of ten years of study and agitation.

The Hindu groups forming the congress party in India, stimulated by the education which they had received under Britain's rule and by the example of British authority and law and system which they had been taught to admire, have demanded an ever-increasing power for themselves in their government. The problem was terribly complicated for a population three times the population of the United States and of a variety and diversity of language, religion, custom unknown in the United States had all to be considered. One-fourth of the population was under the sway of native princes in native States, some of these princes having granted to their subjects a modicum of self-rule. Three-fourths were in the British State, but these three-fourths included millions of Mohammedans and Sikhs: hostile, bitterly contending races for which it was plainly impossible to prescribe the simple methods which are workable in Great Britain. The turning point was reached when, at the first of the three conferences held in London, the princes signified their readiness to come into a federal government for all India.

Mahatma Gandhi, the homely, emaciated leader, greatly gifted in spiritual power, but with a limited outlook in political matters, for a time made the settlement more difficult. He has now retired from politics, devoting himself to his spiritual work, particularly to the protection and elevation of the outcast classes, the depressed classes which have for centuries been the despised and oppressed underdogs in Indian life. But, miraculous to observe, these depressed, outcast classes are to be guaranteed full representation in the new Indian government. The details of it are too complicated for short exposition. Enough for us to know that Great Britain has for that enormous Asiatic dependency accepted the obligation to cultivate among its multiform peoples the power and the habit of self-government, to withdraw in rapid, progressive stages the overlordship of British rulers, always with a determination, however, not to permit the racial and religious feuds to get control of the situation and to reduce India to a Chinese chaos.

The significant fact is that not the Labor Party and the Liberal Party but the Conservative Party is pushing this scheme to consummation. Naturally enough a section of that party, headed by Winston Churchill, has been bitterly hostile, but Stanley Baldwin, the typical John Bull, has been persistent. All the processes of examination and formulation, of discussion and dispute essential to such a monster undertaking have been gone through. The joint committee of the House of Lords and the House of Commons has reported. The law is now before the Commons and will undoubtedly be enacted. Even the House of Lords, almost without a division, when it had heard Lord Reading, the ex-viceroy, expound the difficulties of the situation, the impossibility of continuing to rule 350 million Hindus and Mohammedans with a handful of 135,000 British residents, consented to the principle of the measure.

So Britain remains not only faithful to its old form of government, but is aggressively spreading that form around the world.

Now look at the steps which have been taken in the home land for adjusting social life and economic organization to the difficulties, to the maladjustments that have arisen through the industrial revolution, maladjustments which have been the main cause of the desperate surrender of democracy in foreign lands. England also has suffered; unemployment has been large and long continued. The shipyards on the Tyne and on the Clyde have been silent. The coal industry has been half destroyed. The condition of the country has been desperate. And yet no riots, no uprisings, no Fascist movement, no demand for the overthrow of everything! Why is this? Because England has for seventy-five years been getting ready for this crisis. It is seventy-five years at least since the doctrine began to be rejected that business must be left alone: that the law of supply and demand, the rule of unlimited competition must be free to work out their own fell purposes.

Away back in the middle of the nineteenth century prophets like Carlyle and Ruskin and Kingsley first stirred the British conscience to a realization of the devilish results to humanity of leaving the economic system unregulated, uncoordinated, not brought under a social control. Away back seventy-five years ago they began tentatively in shops and factories and stores in England to establish some democratic control of the processes of production. It is over forty years since the great work of Beatrice and Sidney Webb revealed to us young welfare workers and reformers in London the extent and success of the unionization of industry in England and Scotland. Contrast their cotton industry, for instance, with the American cotton industry. Already forty years ago every last man and woman employed in cotton mills was also in the labor union. Every last employer was in the employers' association. Already the union was managed with such statesmanship and power that its officers, its walking delegates, the men who daily negotiated with the employers, were selected by a civil service system. Examinations for proficiency were applied with the same rigor and effectiveness as in the civil service system of the imperial government. All through Lancashire the great cotton mills in every township towered above the low mean residences of the workers, as feudal castles towered from their rocky heights over the dwellings of the retainers at the foot. But these cotton workers in Lancashire had a dignity unknown, unsuspected by the feudal serfs, for they had a union which spoke on equal terms with the employers' association. Did that result in inequality? Did it mean the destruction of the industry? Not at all. The employers found that they were all on the same footing as to wages and conditions of labor. They would no more dream of trying to make arbitrary wage rates with individuals than they would dream of setting, without negotiations or contract, the price of the raw materials which they purchase.

Practically all industry in England is unionized. The exceptions are insignificant. These unions hold their annual parliament, which is an important conclave, reported by the press, watched to learn how the mind of the proletariat is moving.

Towards the end of the century the great mining leader, Keir Hardie, conceived the idea that labor should use its economic power and its power of organization to win political influence, and then use that political influence for the forwarding of its economic program. And the Labor Party in the nineties came into existence. I was in on it personally. I was chairman of the Labor Party in one of the great boroughs of London, with a population of 250,000, in the government of which we took an active part. I knew James Ramsay Mac-Donald, and frequently sat down with him to a fifteen- to twenty-five-cent supper in an A. B. C. tearoom, he finding it inconvenient just then to produce more than the fifteen cents. What a far cry to 1935, when, as he said in jest, the duchesses all want to kiss him, and Lord and Lady Londonderry, the leaders of British society, have adopted him as their protege and shower him with all the delights, the fascinations, and the temptations which English society has always known how to utilize for the subjection of recalcitrant or radical men of power!

The Labor Party came into existence. It had one main purpose: utilization of the political authority for the remodeling of the economic business life. It has twice controlled the government. Neither time was it able to institute any very drastic changes. It was overthrown the last time because England's industry is absolutely dependent upon foreign trade. When Threadneedle Street quivered, when the gold basis was shattered, all England was aghast. It is impossible in England to carry through drastic reorganization except after consideration of the effects on foreign trade. Foreign trade is the life-blood of Britain. So the Socialist Party and the trade unions are always strictly limited. They may never make the cost of production too high to permit the lavish export of British products. At present there is going forward a dispute as to whether English Socialism shall strive for a swift Marxian overthrow or be content with the inevitability of gradualness, as Sidney Webb phrased it. One section, headed by Sir Stafford Cripps and the Socialist League demands that a radical program be immediately developed, that when the Labor Party comes once more to power it shall proceed ruthlessly, instantly, to put that radical program into effect. In the autumn of 1934 the subject was debated at the conventions of both the Labor Party and the Trade Union Party. In both, the moderates trounced the radicals. All idea of dictatorship of the proletariat was renounced. Fascism and Communism alike were heartily condemned. Both groups laid down the rule that changes must be constitutional, that the population must be first converted to approval of any schemes to change and adjust. The schemes must be put into effect without bloodshed.

They are encouraged in this view by the great strides already made. To one who was brought up in England, who has seen the transformations being made year by year with almost universal approval, it is somewhat amusing to notice the emotional antagonism stirred in America towards Rooseveltian proposals which are already out of date in Great Britain. A great system for social security has already for decades been in operation. Old age pensions, health insurance, workingmen's compensation, unemployment insurance: these have already in England lifted the standard of life so that in London the ten per cent which Charles Booth's survey showed to be below the poverty line in the late nineties has been eliminated and the new survey going forward has already demonstrated that the most oppressed and poverty-stricken classes of London, numbering an appalling multitude at the end of the last century, have already been raised to a level of decent livelihood. It is true that in South Wales, in north England, in Scotland, on the banks of the Clyde, there are depressed and distressed areas, worse off than they ever were before. But even to them comes hope, for they also benefit from these beneficent insurance and pension schemes. True, the pensions have none of the Townsendian luxuriance so popular in the United States just now. About five dollars a week is allowed to a man or woman of seventy, but I have seen how that five dollars is a lifesaver.

So England—all England, practically—although that country was the classic home of capitalism, has repudiated the doctrine of *laissez-faire*, let things go along, keep business out of governmental control. There is no class in England now left that would seriously contemplate the return to the methods of the mid-nineteenth century, no important faction that would call for the complete withdrawal of government from business. Every year, even under conservative governments, the reorganization of business goes forward under the ægis of Westminster. In 1926 a bill was passed under which all the development of electrical power in the country was put under public ownership and control and operation. The conservative government recently reintroduced the bill for the public acquisition, operation, and development of the whole internal transportation of London, including subways, street railways, bus systems, every agency by which the population moves around the streets. When Mr. Herbert Morrison, the Minister of Transport in the MacDonald government, first introduced a bill for accomplishing this purpose, he was so unfortunate as to declare that this was the greatest instalment of Socialism ever proposed at one time in any country. Whereupon the opposition became vociferous and more negotiations had to go forward. The labor leaders of the employees on these different forms of transportation were somewhat dubious about the measure; but, finally, a conservative government enacted it into law.

And so England is stated by an authoritative writer in that sedate periodical, *Foreign Affairs,* to be midway between capitalism and socialism. American proposals under the New Deal have many of them been already put into practice with respect to English agriculture. One of the effects of the sway unlimited of the competitive capitalist system was that the countryside of Great Britain was devastated; great areas were thrown out of cultivation; the production of food was rendered unprofitable; the farmers were reduced to penury. The Great War taught the British people that it was not well to sacrifice agriculture, without limit, to the interests of manufacturers. And so now wheat and sugarbeets and dairy products and beef and the like are all subsidized. No longer are they dependent upon the free operation of the law of supply and demand and free inter national trade.

In their subsidized home building the British have been daring, courageous to an extent which we are now beginning to emulate. Since the Great War over one million homes have been erected, aided by public subsidies either central or local. And now a new great housing scheme is being put through the Commons, which contemplates in a series of years the erection of as many as twenty-five million homes under government promotion and support,—figures which even our New Dealers cannot surpass.

The unemployment insurance system has developed under the Conservative as well as the Liberal and Labor governments—the dole system, as we inaccurately style it. Britain discovered that many of the unemployed were unemployable. It had been the practice in England since the days of good Queen Bess to have relief of the destitute administered locally. It was found that this local administration under the new conditions, when great sums were being handed to the unemployed, was inefficient, lax, too generous. And so within a month or two the whole administration of relief, whether through unemployment funds or through poor relief funds, has been taken over by the central authority. No man or woman who is worthy, who is willing to work, who will accept a job when offered, shall be permitted to starve or freeze. But the rare man who lies back, content to be a supine recipient, shall be treated with severity. That system went into effect only a few months ago, late in 1934. It was discovered to be extremely difficult. The administration in certain respects broke down. The Minister of Labor, Lord Stanley, admitted in the House of Commons in January, 1935, that the administration had failed in some localities and would have to be revamped. He "ate crow" so heartily that Lady Astor got angry with him and chided him for showing such a good appetite for crow and giving the Labor opposition a chance to gloat over his discomfiture.

For us the essential thing to notice is that a constant effort is going forward, year in and year out, to reconstruct the economic system, to make it yield greater social and human welfare, to guarantee to the British individual not merely an abstract right to life but a concrete opportunity to live. So democracy is justifying itself in the sight of all people.

I have said that all home generosity is limited by the necessity to make home products cheap enough to enter into foreign commerce.

That brings us to a short consideration of England's international democratic policies. To England the command of the seas has for centuries been a tradition. That is not merely a patriotic jingo claim: the whole life of England has been built up for centuries upon the assumptions of empire and of foreign commerce. In part England is paying a high price today for these past methods. But there it is, inescapable. And so "Britannia Rules the Waves" has not been a mere vaunt of a prideful people. It has been an essential of their lives. But the United States rose to power. The elder daughter of the British family of nations, who had left home early, grew to unexampled might and glory. Great Britain had to determine whether her rule over the waters should be shared with or should be asserted against this newcomer. Decades since they began thinking this matter over; old Sir John Fisher, their most powerful and beloved admiral, before the Great War, had advised the government never to enter into competitive navy building with the United States. So, when Secretary Hughes and President Harding summoned the first naval conference and showed a marvelous, most laudable spirit of conciliation and agreement, it was easy for the two mightiest powers on earth to agree together that the command of the seas should be shared, that neither should have a navy to dominate the other, that both should have navies strong enough to protect their interests.

Japan likewise had to be taken into that agreement because Japan also was becoming a great sea power. Japan has since denounced the naval agreement, and the whole subject is up for reconsideration.

Under those circumstances what is the attitude of the far-sighted, wise, controlling leaders of Great Britain towards the United States? It has been voiced most effectively twice in the last two or three months by the elder statesman of South Africa, General Jan Christian Smuts.

Smuts was a South African, educated at Cambridge, England, a lawyer of ability, a scholar worthy of his Alma Mater. In the Boer War, that wicked effort to subjugate the republics of South Africa, Smuts fought like a lion for his homeland and his home people. British might conquered, but a liberal government recognized that the conquest was rather a disgrace, and that this people must not be destroyed, but must be aided to govern themselves and to become an independent dominion. Smuts took an active part in the establishment of the South African government. When the Great War broke out the effect of this benevolent and far-sighted policy was evident, for the great generals of South Africa, who had previously fought from hill to hill against the British army, with equal bravery and equal skill ranged themselves alongside the Tommies from England to fight Germany. Smuts was an influential negotiator at the peace conference. After the war a division sprang up in South Africa between the Dutch Party and the British Party. The Dutch Party under Hertzog wished to move towards severance from the British empire; the British Party, under Smuts, contended that all the liberties desired were obtainable within the British family of nations. Early in 1935 that conflict was settled. Prime Minister Hertzog has announced that he has no longer any interest in a republic or republicanism. South Africa is united once again under the policy which Smuts has through the decades advocated.

You will readily understand that a man with that record is listened to in Britain. When Smuts speaks Whitehall and Westminster strain their ears. And what has Smuts said which has commanded the grateful attention of the people of England? He says:

"Europe will cease to be the world's center of disturbance, and the center of gravity of world affairs will in the future pass to the Pacific." He remarks with approval that Captain Anthony Eden, the Lord Privy Seal, one of those new brilliant young men who are now adorning British government, declared the other day that "It is one of the special objects of the present British government to develop relations of a close, cordial friendship with the United States of America."

"There can be no doubt," General Smuts continues, "that the success of such a policy is ardently desired by the British people as a whole, and even more by the young nations of the Commonwealth. The dominions have a fundamental sympathy with the United States of America and desire nothing more than a close collaboration with her in world affairs.

"For their own future security they look partly to the U. S. A. They feel sure that what happened in the Great War will happen again in any grave crisis of the future and that in the hour of danger these two groups will be found side by side, treaty or no treaty. The call of instinct and fundamental affinities will be far stronger than any written document could.

"While this is so, the question yet arises whether the situation now threatening the Far East does not call for some more tangible sign of cooperation on the part of the U. S. A. If Japan knew that, treaty or no treaty, there was in fact a policy of practical cooperation between the British and American groups, that knowledge would in all probability itself suffice to insure the peace of the Pacific."

Britannia says to Columbia: "I have shared with you my trident and the rule of the waves; I now proffer the hand of maternal affection." And what will Columbia's answer be? Certain groups, influential, clamorous, will spurn the proffer. The same mass of militant fighters who overthrew the World Court in the United States Senate will disdain the hand of England. William Randolph Hearst and his Arthur Brisbane, whose message reaches millions of homes at every breakfast table, will sedulously foment discord. "We make no friends; we defy all foes" will be their motto. They will continue to demand that America make itself impregnable by force and repel all association with other countries. They assert that every treaty concerning armaments is an infringement of sovereignty. They want no other method than the building and more building of airplanes and ships and the equipment of ever-larger armies. They will ask that the United States repudiate the treaties of London and of Washington and join Japan in declaring that for the future they will be limited by no agreements. They will demand that the United States carry out a program of such magnitude in airplane building that the very heavens will be darkened by the avenging angels of America. They will suggest that on the Atlantic coast the United States should have a navy strong enough to defy the navy of Great Britain, that on the Pacific coast the United States should have another navy strong enough to defy the navy of Japan, and these belligerent claims will be iterated and reiterated with abominable persistence.

What will the rest of the people do while that campaign is going forward? We cannot escape our responsibilities. Having made it our policy to float a navy second to none it is impossible for us to withdraw from negotiations with Great Britain, except at the cost of adopting some such program as I have outlined. And so you and I, as well as the British people, are at a fateful turning-point. It is not simply my blood that prompts me to recommend a sympathetic consideration of this proffer of British cooperation. It is no longer possible to say, with respect to navies: "We will do our own will regardless of the will or wishes of other peoples." We can maintain our independence in foreign policy. We may disagree with Smuts as to the dangers in the Western Pacific. He may find himself incorrect in his assumption that the integrity of China is part of the fundamental foreign policy of the United States. We are not called upon to commit ourselves as to our policies in years to come. But the naval treaties are there; they expire two years hence; the decision must be made. We can't avoid determining whether we will have friendship or hostility. Smuts says that if England and America simply let Japan know that they would walk side by side in the future, Japan would soon cease to be a menace. We have to choose either to walk side by side or to pull wider apart. Pulling apart we give Japan's military clique its great opportunity for dominion. Clasping hands we assure the world for a long period against a naval war.

You and I as part of this democracy are confronted with an obligation, with a duty. To us the challenge comes: "Choose ye this day whom ye will serve. If the Lord be God, then follow him; if Baal or Hearst, then follow him."

CHAPTER X

Democracy

in

the

United States

CHAPTER X

Democracy in the United States: Life, Liberty, the Pursuit of Happiness

THE foundations of the foreign policy of the United States were laid by Washington and Jefferson when they uttered two phrases which have been frequently recited. Washington said: "The great rule of conduct for us in regard to foreign nations is in extending our commercial relations, to have with them as little political connection as possible." Thomas Jefferson put the same more briefly: "Peace, commerce, and honest friendship with all nations; entangling alliances with none." Emphasis has most often been laid upon the negative aspects of these two injunctions: "entangling alliances with none" and "as little political connection as possible." Historically, in practice, the positive aspect has been more important: "extending our commercial relations to foreign nations", "commerce with all nations". That was assumed from the beginning to be a fundamental part of the policy of the American Republic. Almost immediately the American flag flew in ports around the world. Commerce unrestricted, independent, had been one of the main claims in the revolt against British rule; and this right of extended commerce over all the oceans speedily was asserted in practice. A mercantile marine was constructed to carry that commerce, so that in the decades preceding the Civil War the American clippers, as graceful as gulls, as speedy as the eagle, competed for supremacy on the waters, often winning the prize for the first arrival in London of the early cargoes of tea from the new crops in China.

In the Civil War this commerce in the southern ports was destroyed, but in the northern ports it expanded. The Civil War then, as the "Great War" later, called for increasing exports and imports, and New York rose to supremacy. After the Civil War, when the mercantile marine changed from wood to steel, the American people were so busy expanding across the continent, building new railroads, establishing factories and industries, that the provision of ships of the new types did not attract them, and when the Great War burst on the world American commerce was impeded. Insufficient bottoms under the American flag could be found to make up the deficiencies when British and other foreign ships were withdrawn from service. When America entered the war new bottoms were urgently called for. "Ships must win the war," as well as half a dozen other factors.

So at Hog Island the American mass method of production of vessels was tried. Before they could be put afloat the war closed, and so they lay for years after, fleets of them, resting at anchor off Staten Island and up the Hudson, where I often gazed upon them, the melancholy remnants of war waste. However, the trade continued to increase until exports and imports reached the stupendous totals each year of nine to ten billion dollars. Who should provide the vessels in which to carry that trade? American private initiative and sturdy individualism shirked the task. It said, "We cannot reap enough profits from this business. The government must go into and once more further this commerce which it has fostered sedulously from the republic's birthday." That indicated a change of national psychology which had been accelerated by the war experiences. We shall see the effects of that change of psychology upon domestic policies later. Enough to realize that under President Coolidge a system of ship aids was established in the form of cheap loans for seventy-five per cent of the cost of building a vessel and heavy postal rates, known to be several times the cost of the service, established deliberately to foster an American marine.

Now, this week (March, 1935), President Roosevelt proposes a continuation in a new form of these State aids to commerce. The Republicans having done it, the Democrats continuing and enlarging it, the vote is unanimous. Sturdy individualism, private initiative, dependence upon the enterprise of the private capitalists all subordinated, brought under a new rule, the rule that the government must actively co-operate in these enterprises. All through the history of the republic, as a matter of course, consulates and ambassador-ships were established round the world for the purpose of stimulating and guiding this commerce as it was pursued by private American citizens. It was for that end, mainly, that our navy was constructed. It was for that purpose that we dared the risks of war, and that again we may be brought to war, if we insist on asserting the old rights of freedom of the seas in time of war as in time of peace, as we did up to 1917. That aspect of it we can postpone to later consideration. We must hurry on to consider the domestic policies and their foundations, with which, of course, the foreign commerce has always been intertwined.

It is frequently, but, I think, inaccurately stated that the domestic economic system, like Topsy, has "just growed", without specific guidance, without known and formulated aims. That is far from the truth. The United States govern-ment has frequently, sometimes with enormous force, as-serted itself for the development of national economic plans. Ours has not been a planless economy. We have frequently put brains and efforts into deciding the course we wanted our economic life to follow. Henry Clay had a platform of inter-nal improvements and tariff statutes. What for? Internal improvements meant the building of the road over the Cum-berland gap, the construction of canals, the deliberate encour-agement of transportation and of migration. The tariff was debated with the aim of establishing a system under which this country should be changed in part from an agricultural to an industrial nation, as deliberately, after longer debates and for the same ultimate purpose, as the Five-Year Plan in Russia. Naturally, under the sway of purely economic forces, this country would have remained agricultural, predominantly, with industry only an insignificant part of the national life.

In the forties and fifties of the last century the industrial magnates and financial leaders, as well as the plain people, determined that the economic life should be operated in future by free men, and not by slaves. That was a colossal interference with the operation of economic law. It involved consequences of tremendous import. The North had discovered by experience that free labor was more advantageous than slave labor, at any rate under the conditions of northern climate and northern agriculture. The South would not accept that economic conclusion, although some convincing books demonstrated it. Emotional, human, religious principles became involved. The matter was not settled, unfortunately, by economic reason and agreement; but calamitously by war. Despite the reluctance of the Southern States to change over their economy, to plan it on a different system, the North in a bloody contest forced its will upon them.

President Lincoln had been elected partly by virtue of the development of another economic plan. The wage-earners of the North wanted the Homestead Act, which would give to them the opportunity to escape ill-paid labor in eastern cities and to take up quarter sections of land as free gifts of the government. The manufacturers wanted tariffs on many articles, that their baby industries might grow in strength. The two combined and won their double purpose,—a deliberate effort to balance industry and agriculture to the profit of both.

Later another great step in the planning of American industrial life was taken by the establishment of corporations. It had been in the beginning the almost universal rule that agriculture and industry were conducted by individuals and partners, with individual or joint responsibility. The establishments changed hands at the death of the owner or the partner. That was found ineffective for the greater enterprises which the growth of the country required. So the political government began to establish by its own side, subordinate to it in some respects, independent of it in other respects, an economic government operating through these creatures of the State, the corporations.

I think we shall be aided in understanding our present

economic dilemma if we realize that every factory involves government. When a man is working on his own, either on the farm or in the workshop, he is his own master; he can follow his own desires, he can abandon his work when he wishes to take an afternoon off fishing. He is actually, in his day's labor, a free man. But the moment fifty or a hundred men are gathered by an entrepreneur under one roof and put to work cooperatively in production a government is established. The boss gives orders which must be obeyed. He lays out plans which must be executed. He is captain of a producing force, and the private must obey his directions.

That system worked smoothly and comfortably in the main so long as the captain was there on the job, in contact with the privates, cultivating friendly relations with them. They all realized they were doing a cooperative task. But in proportion as, through the expansion of industry, establishments grew in size, and the governing heads left the factory sites and were placed in cities far away, the rulership remained, but the relations changed. Always there was an uneasy sense, on the part of the workers, that they were being controlled in the most important matters of their lives, their day's labor, by persons or forces away off, with whom there could be no contact, whose decisions could not be discussed by them, who had no intimate awareness of the human elements in their establishments, who were a government without immediate responsibiliy, analagous to, although in important respects differing from, the government of feudal lords over their distant serfs.

The State has gone on granting these corporate franchises, under which the establishments enjoy a perpetual life. They never die. The corporation endures after all the original members have been put in their graves. They are entrusted by the community with the performance of avowedly important duties in the life of the community. They are entrusted with special powers to enable them to perform those duties, but the corresponding responsibilities and obligations to the community have up to the present been only dimly recognized.

We have created deliberately a government within a government, a young government which has become, without anybody willing it in any evil manner, a small oligarchy, so that we have today two hundred corporations that control the output of fifty-one per cent or more of all industry.

We have a concentrated financial control which has come fortuitously into being that can affect the lives of tens of thousands of American citizens more intimately than can the legislatures of a dozen States. That authority has been exercised, in the main, in accordance with the principles, the fundamentals of American democracy. When the elder Morgan met his sub-generals of financial influence in his library on days of panic and threatened disaster, he often acted with magnanimity, with a sense of obligation to the immediate situation entirely admirable. George F. Baker and James Stillman and Morgan and Gary and the rest in charge, at the headquarters of the general staff of industry often realized, in times of stress, their responsibility and did their best to discharge it. They made blunders from which the rest of the world suffered. When J. P. Morgan bought up at extravagant prices all the competitors of the New York, New Haven & Hartford Railroad, he ruined thousands of families along that road. People who had been living in proud opulence, imagining that they were safe for the remainder of their days, were brought to want. They had no remedy. An error committed by those leaders of the economic oligarchy was more fateful to them than any taxes laid in Connecticut, and yet there has been little realization that we do have this government, and the people who have suffered under it have not found any remedy. Taxation without representation was concentrated into one issue which was fought out against the tyranny of King George; but ruin without representation has started no war to remedy it.

That was the government, the inefficient demoralized government, the government operating only partly within law, which broke down in 1929 and 1930. When President Roosevelt came into power he said, "The people of the United States have not failed. We do not fear for the failure of the principles of our democracy, but the leaders of finance and industry have failed, and we must drive the money-changers out of the temple." Perhaps that was a little unjust. The leaders have not been made conscious of their responsibilities; there has been no codification of their duties; they were working in great part at haphazard. It had been supposed that if every man attended to his own profit, the profit of the whole would be assured. And so, in 1933, this democracy was brought face to face with disaster. Disaster had been slowly accumulating. President Hoover had nobly tried to ward it off. It was not a failure of the political powers. Hoover was not to blame. Hoover was caught in a hurricane. He was worn out with his labors. He was baffled and thwarted. The economic powers had lost control of their machinery. Forces had been set running which they could not stem, and so in March, 1933, the nation called to the White House: "Save us, or we perish." That cry went up not only from the workmen who were suffering; it went up from the leaders themselves. Other nations had faced this dilemma, brought on during the same period. Other nations had schemed and failed. Other nations said in effect, "We can't do it. Give us a dictator. We will submit to anything, if only you will save us from this starvation, anxiety, and misery."

The American people made no such demand as a people, although it is said that the President of the Chamber of Commerce of the United States did call for a dictator, and General Hugh Johnson relates that only the reluctance, the steady refusal of Roosevelt to assume such an obnoxious role prevented the establishment of a dictatorship at that time. I can hardly credit it, but that is General Johnson's statement of two nights ago (March 5, 1935).

We were forced, then, to face the situation. We entered upon a century's labor of reconstruction. We started with a great rush. We were determined to take the castle in one rapid assault. But we are finding, and we shall find more and more, that the labors must be continued; neither faint-heartedness nor hurry will restore prosperity and maintain prosperity. We shall have to gird up our loins for a long march before we reach the promised land.

Let us look next at some of the fundamentals which the American democracy instinctively discovers on starting out on this long task. First, as I have hinted, it is a national job, not a party job. In Italy and Germany the national aspect has been reached by the extermination of all opposing or critical parties. We cannot and will not pursue that method, but we must by some means obtain a similar union of purpose, or we shall be defeated. Our party system calls for certain customary opposition and criticism. That we can easily endure. Perhaps six or eight years hence the Republican Party will return to power; but the problem will remain. Life must go on, and America, like the other countries of the world, must adjust its machinery to make that life prosperous, whatever political party is ascendant. Next, it cannot be done by a dictator, as I have already indicated. Next, it cannot be accomplished through the waging of any class war. We know no such classes. It is one of the glories of America that classes are not fossilized; the workman is not committed, doomed to be forever a workman. There is a career open to talent, and we cannot make our reconstruction upon the Marxian basis that there is an irreconcilable conflict between wage-earners and employers. Mr. William Green, President of the American Federation of Labor, said recently that the automobile workers had been robbed to make the fortunes of the millionaires who had been created in the motor industry. That is his expression of the Marxian doctrine of surplus value. It isn't correct! The workers are not the only and sometimes not the chief sufferers from our chaos. The investors have been robbed just as much as the workers. This is not a case for the preletarians alone to protest; J. P. Morgan's firm lost twenty million dollars, and many thousands have lost their substance, their reliance for old age. Many thousands who have been socially above the proletariat have suffered more intensely in mind, through anxiety and anguish on account of the uncertainty of the future, than has the workman. He was frequently so accustomed to uncertainty that he had never anticipated the conditions of life decades in advance.

So this is a problem to be solved by democracy on cooperative democratic principles. It cannot be solved in our country upon the Socialist method, which is, "let the government own and run everything." We are not equipped to own and run everything. That does not mean that we may take no step in any direction when the public interest is to be conserved by national action, but the unique method of Socialism—government ownership and operation—is not applicable to our conditions.

That leads me to dilate a little on the advantages and disadvantages of the American form and spirit of democracy, compared with democracies elsewhere. We enjoy a social solidarity, at any rate outside of the few big cities on the eastern seaboard, that "a man's a man for a' that!"—a readiness to combine, a swiftness in meeting an emergency.

I remember that once I was conveying an English guest along an Adirondack road. I was trying to bring home to him this social democracy that prevails throughout America—fully west of the Alleghenies, to a considerable extent east of the Alleghenies. Just then a man held up his hand to stop us. We got out of our car, and we found that a lady had run her car aside into mud and was bogged. It needed a little combination of man force to drag her out. And so, as a matter of course, every man who came along the road in a car was stopped, no matter what his social state or worth, no matter what clothes he wore, or how learned he might be; he was a man, and here was an emergency. So we all jumped out. One person produced a rope. Another took charge, just by virtue of his power in leadership and his mastery of the situation. The rope was tied to the car; we all took hold, and with one "heave, ho!" the difficulty was overcome.

Now that couldn't happen in just that way in Great Britain. And that spirit of mutual helpfulness is going to be our main standby in the difficult years ahead.

Next, we have an alert scientific leadership which is looking for means of stabilizing industry. I think we shall discover our key for ourselves, in all probability; we can't borrow a key from Europe. We are finding, and Henry Ford is announcing, through megaphones heard around the world, that mass production must be supplemented with mass consumption. That is a necessity of industry, and mass consumption means higher wages, a wider distribution of consuming power. We are slowly turning our minds to put that doctrine into effect. It's not easy; it can't be done overnight; but I think Marx was correct to this extent: that it is the development of industry itself and its necessities which compel fundamental changes. That fundamental change, mass consumption, will be a requisite result of the change to mass production which was undertaken fortuitously, which has been extended throughout industry, and which cannot be abandoned for small production and for any return to hand methods.

Next, what disadvantages does American democracy labor under? First, our political representatives do not include, by and large, except in the highest places, the best brains or character of the population. We have an unfortunate habit of despising our rulers. Nobody is held by Will Rogers to be fairer prey for his rapier than the House of Congress. That attitude of mind and that condition of affairs has both an advantageous and a disadvantageous side; it has a disadvantageous side in that it has kept out of politics, on the average, the best minds. Only occasionally do we capture an intellectual and natural aristocrat for political position, because to his other qualities he must add the ability of the vote-getter. That is difficult, almost impossible to acquire for many of those who are equipped with the other valuable powers. On the other hand, our government is part of ourselves as it is not anywhere else in the world. Professor Gustaf Stolper, one of the brainiest, I think, of the German refugees, has pointed out that the government in the United States means to the people something quite different from what the government means to any people in Europe. Our government is not Ruler So-and-so; he is just Bill Smith. He is not the High Counselor Muck-a-muck; he is just Tom Jones, with whom we used to go fishing. Our government is closely allied to us.

I had a striking illustration of that distinction when Mme. Maxim Gorki was my guest. She would go into New York City and observe the policemen. At first she assumed that they were Cossacks, there to terrify the multitude. Dimly and slowly she came to the understanding: "Why, they are just friends! I saw a policeman with a man on the elevated road and the man was not cowering and the policeman scowling; they were just talking in a friendly way, just human beings together." So, despite the difference between the economic government and the political government, we have this intimate contact with the political government all up and down which makes it susceptible to the expression of our wishes and the execution of the changes requisite for our well-being. Another serious disability from which we suffer is the Spoils System, unknown in some other democracies today, although known in centuries gone by, the assumption that a man's political merit is to be judged by the number of jobs he can procure for his constituents. That is a terrible handicap. We have only begun to wrestle with it. It took me some years to comprehend the crusading fervor of the civil service reformers, who started their active lives in the days of Cleveland, to comprehend that the Spoils System was the enemy, and that the purification of political life, its efficiency and smooth operation, depend upon getting that Spoils System brought to heel.

With all these conditions immediately immutable, we faced in March, 1933, a devastating crisis. First, like both Hitler and Mussolini, our leader had to restore confidence; the nation was shaken, despairing, disintegrating, uncertain as to what would happen next. The banks had to be closed the country over. Unemployment rose to an amount unprecedented. The nation's heart was broken with fear, and first American morale had to be restored. It was restored. And as Professor Stolper says, American democracy gave the most incontestable proof of its power and efficiency in the whole course of its history. We got together, and for a year we stuck together, and during that year we performed together marvels. First, hunger and want were overcome. The people were assured that an honest man, eager to work, with his resources of a thrifty life exhausted, should not be left helpless to starve and freeze. Hitler did the same, but we also accomplished that task without a dictatorship. We set about reestablishing agriculture. We were under the sway of a new conception of society, the conception which, if not born, was nurtured into full strength during the war, the realization of the capacity of the nation to act collectively. The prodigious feats the nation could accomplish when it did act unitedly had staggered us and revealed to us the possibilities that lay within us, if only we utilized them fully.

We were also under the influence of a scientific spirit which had just begun to come into maturity. We are no longer willing to lie down and be whipped, and to be told that forces which no man can control are bringing us to despair. We have learned that the scientific method applied to problems will perform miracles, and we said: "We will not submit, as did our fathers, to the long periods of distress and suffering that follow necessarily upon letting things alone, leaving nature, human nature, money and credit and unguided impulses to work at haphazard."

The farmers had long been, in part, despairing. The farm bloc in the United States Congress had attempted various methods for the resuscitation of farm life, and we established a new method, started a new experiment on a huge scale. That experiment has, so far, succeeded. For the first time in the history of this or any other nation the farmers have consented *en masse* to bind themselves by contract to fulfil a common obligation. It is a perfect wonder that in the recent election under their code the cotton growers of the South voted almost unanimously for these great new methods of resuscitation. The farmer's income was increased last year seven hundred millions over his income in 1932; the farmer, naturally individualistic, naturally a grumbler, (for he has always at least the weather for a subject,) has learned in the hot fire of experience that he must fuse for some purposes. He is content to try it out, and the control is proceeding with every promise of major success.

Industry was encouraged to organize itself. Industry had complained that the political power hampered it in its operations through the Anti-Trust Law. When the government had chartered these huge corporations they grew through the process of industrial expansion until they became such mighty units that the people were afraid of them. The common man said: "These are monopolies who will oppress us, and will set prices too high to be borne." We tried uniquely to stop that process by enacting Anti-Trust Laws. No other nation did. We said: "We will put a legal enactment in the way of this rising tide." It didn't succeed; it never can succeed. So, when the ruins had to be repaired, we said to industry: "You organize yourselves. You arrange your codes in order that you may operate with efficiency and fairness; but in these codes, there must be provisions for justice all around, justice not only to the owner, but to the wage-earner, and to the consumer." In Italy Mussolini had followed that theory to the limit. He had said: "Industry, of course, must be organized. We must have employers' associations right up from the village to the nation. We must have workers' organizations right up from the village to the capital, but these different organizations must be controlled by the political power, because the political power is the only protector of the common good." We imitated that method to some extent. We put Section 7A into the codes, approving, in principle, the organization of labor in trade unions.

There again, I think, we shall not abjectly imitate Europe. Heartily as I have worked during my lifetime for trade unions and their objects, I do not share the instinctive antagonism to company unions that many display. It is unnecessary to go on the assumption that there is an irreconcilable conflict between wage-earner and management. They can get together, and the company union may prove under proper limitations to be one method by which they can get together. We made a blunder, I think, a characteristically American blunder. Led by the ebullient General Hugh Johnson we said: "We will bring all industry, from the barber shop on the crossroad up to the financial institution in Wall Street suddenly, within three months, under codes, under order, under regulations. We will make one grand rush and finish the job." But, of course, we failed in that. However, a considerable residue of attainment remains. 2,550,000 extra men have been put to work in private industry in two years since March, 1933. Another 2,550,000—curiously enough, the figures are almost the same, if you add them up—have been put to work on relief works and public works of one kind and another; and notice that 2,550,000 is more than the total number of unemployed in Great Britain at the maximum. That's an indication of the magnitude of the job we are forced to try to accomplish.

Again, we started on a great scheme for rectifying the hardships that follow from the operation of our money and credit system. America has been unique in its history, in that it has always been restless under the operations of our money and credit system, and periodically this restlessness has broken out into incipient revolt. I have not thought so previously, but I think today that that dissatisfaction has been a sign of the superior mentality and sounder instinct of the American people. H. G. Wells points out in his new autobiography that when he and I were young men together engaged in reform activities in London, it was always thought that any man who even discussed the money question had wheels in his head; he was almost ready for an asylum. So fixed was the superstition that the existing money system was an unchangeable system, that it could never be altered to advantage. But England has been off the gold standard since that time, and England has become acutely aware of the insanities inherent in the money system. England is questioning, as did the disconsolate Americans in decades gone by, "Why should a farmer who has worked hard all the year, who has been favored by nature, who has grown a full crop, who has rejoiced on the day of harvest, be denied the fruits of his labor by some changes in the world market due to the manipulation of money, perhaps, three thousand miles away? Why should a professional man who has saved religiously, who has lived honorably, who has put his money in so-called securities, find their value dissolved like dew in the morning sunshine through some changes in a money market entirely outside of his ken and entirely outside his control?"

And so we courageously, boldly, some say recklessly, started in to study and try to control in the public interest that money and credit system; for the control of money and credit means control of the masses, and dominant power in trade and indusry. "At any rate," we said, "the farmer and the house-owner who are faced with foreclosure on their properties shall not be left to the unmitigated mercy of the law. The public money which was used so voluminously to aid banks shall also be used to aid farmers and mechanics." On the whole, that has worked to great advantage, and today, materially, the country has revived to a considerable degree. The output of industry last month (February, 1935) was higher than in any month since 1929, except July, 1933. We have recovered our tone to great degree.

But we are beginning to get tired of being good. Divisions are appearing. The consciousness of the nation as one hasn't yet got hold of us. We are so big, so multifarious, so varied, that this sense of national unity is a great deal harder for us to acquire than it would be for the small, homogeneous population of England; and criticisms, sometimes unfair, sometimes disconcertingly selfish, are appearing from the right and from the left. The right says: "Stop this spending. Let's return to the good old American method." And they fancy that the good old American method means government doing nothing about it. They haven't read history, or they could labor under no such delusion. If you argue with them, you can say: "Well, according to the good old American method the government should foreclose immediately on its loans to the banks. Half of them would go into the hands of receivers. Is that what you want? The government should call for its money from the insurance companies. Is that what you want? The government should demand that all the railroads immediately meet their obligations, and half of them overnight would go into bankruptcy. Is that what you want?" Because that is not what the people of America want—or will endure. The American people have resolved that they will not submit tamely to the ravages of the economic foe, but that they will apply their mind and their will to the rectifying of the evils that have grown from unregulated, unplanned finance and industry. America is giving a great demonstration of its power and efficiency.

And yet we haven't stirred to enthusiasm the people of the country, especially the young, as Mussolini and Hitler have done. I think we are not bold enough in our imaginings. We are too humble as to what democracy can accomplish. We should shout: "Wherefore do ye doubt, O! ye of little faith?" American democracy has only begun its triumph. We have created on this continent a productive machine unequaled elsewhere, and now we will proceed to master that machine, to make it serve the common good. We cannot endure that ten million men shall stand idle, and ten thousand factories shut down, their furnaces cold, when the men and the factories together could supply the whole country with an abundant life. We are not willing to concede that we can't do it. Nothing that man has done is beyond the power of the American people. And so we ought to say to the young: "You are born in a great age; you are born in a country which has a program far exceeding in splendor the Five-Year program of Communist Russia." Herbert Hoover once dimly adumbrated this idea, but he was caught in the fury of the storm, and nobody showed any interest. If we use our imaginations and see this gladder day, we can say to our young: "We are working for a democratic rule, under which, when the young leave their colleges or their schools, they shall pass naturally and inevitably into work, for which, by that time, they pant. We are working for a democracy which will insure that the devastating botches due to mismanagement of investments and to ill-balanced production shall not recur, and that, when you are fathers, you will not be left to see your children crying for food, because you 'can't get work'." We all know that "he takes my life who takes the means whereby I live." We are guaranteed in our revered Declaration of Independence the inalienable right to life, so we must be guaranteed the inalienable right to work, the right to a job. That right, the twentieth-century form of the right to life, we are determined that democracy shall win. We are striving for a democracy in which the worthy aged shall always be cared for. We expect that, as the years go by, an increasing proportion of the population may come down in their old age to enjoy the benignant influences of Florida's sunshine and health-giving air. And we shall do all this while holding fast to the faith of our forefathers, maintaining that spiritual freedom which we hold dear, sacrificing not one iota of our political independence nor of our right to free thought and expression; for we know that spiritual growth must accompany material growth for the development of a rounded civilization.

All this glory we know we can attain. You young people need not hunger after the flesh pots of Russia. They are empty of sustenance, compared with the banquet that will be spread for you here in America, a banquet intellectual and cultural as well as material. For, along with economic regeneration we are unitedly determined that "this nation, under God, shall have a new birth of freedom and that government of the people, by the people, for the people shall not perish from the earth."

CHAPTER XI

Youth

and

Dictatorships

CHAPTER XI

Youth and Dictatorships

A Challenge to Patriotism and the Leadership of Youth in America

Address delivered at Knowles Memorial Chapel,
Rollins College, May 12, 1935.

ONE of the most startling and unexpected features of the dictatorships which sway Russia, Italy, and Germany today is the enthusiastic support which is given them by the youth of the countries. Criticism and opposition, where raised at all, are voiced mainly, almost exclusively, by the mature, the aged. The youth are spurred to cheerful enthusiasm. Not because the youth are pampered and petted, for endurance and service are demanded from them.

In Russia the Young Communists are held on call for the relief of lumber camps in the arctic regions, for rapid aid with labor in the darkness of the Don coal mines, for sweeping trips into the harvest regions, for doing and suffering.

In Germany, when on March 16th, military conscription was announced to be reestablished, the edict was received, not with whining but with acclamation. The young rose and cheered.

When Mussolini issues a call for troops to go to Abyssinnia, there to endure the agonies of thirst in the desert, the hardship of long marches with heavy packs, the dangers of fighting with savage, resolute, black men, the suffering of wounds and death,—the young Black Shirts of the Fascist militia offer no resistance. They leap forward, ready to endure, to suffer, to die.

How comes it that, with ideals largely barbarous, with military purposes supreme, the youth of dictatorships put to shame the youth of our democracy in their willingness to serve? The phenomenon may be explained by two factors:

215

First, the dictatorships organize and propagandize their ideal of the State. They have positive convictions. They do not shilly-shally and advise this creed this day and another another day. They do not fill the land with criticism and fault-finding. The dictators know what they want. They call upon the youth assiduously, tirelessly, to accept the State faith of the leaders; and youth responds to the expression of deep conviction. Hitler in his labor camps puts before the eyes of all the youth such signs as: "Thy people are everything. You, individually, are nothing." "We were born to die for Germany." Devilish doctrine as it seems to us—"born to die for Germany"! Not born to live for Germany, not born to make a better Germany; but born to die in battle for Germany. That summons to sacrifice does not terrify young Germans. They respond joyously.

Second, in each dictatorship an ideal of State has been formulated and announced, an ideal of national unity which contains some fine features, and calls the individual from selfish absorption in his own welfare to a realization of the millions of his fellow citizens—a brotherhood based on nationality and race, or in Russia, on community of belief. In each case the dictator promises to bring to all his citizens a fuller material life. These promises have been only partially kept. Perhaps it was impossible to keep them in a decade. But the promises inspired the young. Hitler said last winter: "No German shall freeze or starve." The whole German people shall be one people to the extent that no individual in the national family shall be left helpless. That promise he redeemed.

Stalin inspires his youth by a picture of an earthly paradise which is to be attained by whole-hearted devotion to the Communist Party and the teachings of its leaders. In doing this the dictators, while sometimes repudiating religion and denying God, have seized upon one of the fundamental doctrines of the Christian religion, that he who loseth his life shall find it; that happiness comes through duty fulfilled to human beings outside oneself, outside even of one's family.

We in democratic America have not yet caught the force

of that doctrine, and have not organized it in the State. We have few formulated ideas of State obligation. The best among us have been afraid to preach patriotism, because patriotism has been identified almost exclusively with militarism. When the war broke out the government at once treated us, we treated each other, shall I say, as one nation. The most poverty-stricken, ignorant, degraded share croppers in the deepest South were not too far away from Washington to be reached by the drafting board. For war purposes everybody was expected to serve, and America discovered, what the countries of Europe also discovered, that, in the mass, the youth, convinced that it was serving some higher cause than its own selfish interests, did enthusiastically leap to the breach.

But peace time patriotism is pallid and anemic. A visitor from Mars would think that patriotism means shifting the taxes to the other fellow. We have seemed to be afraid to call upon our youth for valor in peace time; for patriotic service in anything but war. Nobody in official power has formulated the modern American ideal for which youth might be summoned to service. Yet, surely, Democracy has visions more glorious than Hitler's or Mussolini's.

Suppose some great leader should arise who would venture to present to American youth the ideal for which America stands, the ideal to which American youth are asked to consecrate themselves. How would he build it?

In contradistinction to the dictators, he would begin by saying that the foundation of American thought is the doctrine of the supreme value of the individual soul, a doctrine which is a fundamental principle of Christianity. In politics the correlative doctrine is the fundamental value of the individual citizen—humanity before either State or property. The State exists ultimately for the individual, for his protection, his service, the organization of certain of his activities. Not at all that the individual owes no obligation to the State; but that the discharge of this obligation will redound, ultimately, to the good of the individual, who must be the final beneficiary. Not State expansion but individual development is the goal.

The leader would show that America will not sacrifice human soul values for State aggrandizement; that it will sustain inviolate those freedoms and forms of government which have become a consecrated part of American tradition and history. He might use the words employed last Thursday (May 9th) by King George V in answering the addresses of loyalty and devotion of the Lords and Commons. The United States, like the United Kingdom, means "government by the people, freedom for the individual, ordered strength of State, and the rule of law over governors and governed alike." America's social organization is based upon the magnificent assertion: Every man is endowed with certain inalienable rights, among which are life, liberty and the pursuit of happiness. Life, an inalienable right! Therefore, in America, more fully than in a dictatorship, no man or woman who is willing to work shall by ill-luck or denial of opportunity be deprived of his life.

Not that the State owes every man a living; but that the State, the coöperative community, owes to every man the opportunity to earn a living. The right to live involves the right to work; for "he takes my life who takes the means whereby I live." So complicated has our industrial system become that the individual is only a cog in a vast machine and when that machine slows down or stops his right to life is jeopardized. Our ideal leader would boldly announce, with the approval of the majority of the citizens and the unanimous endorsement of youth, that America stands for a job for everybody.

This doctrine would be in harmony with the deep-seated instincts of Americans. No people are more kind-hearted, no business men so tender, at bottom, in their sympathy. As Santayana has written: "If I looked into the heart of any man and found, deep down, cruelty and oppression, I should know that that man was not an American." That deep-seated sympathy with our fellows should be embodied in our institutions, which should provide that no American citizen shall be left, through the accidents of sickness, of economic breakdown, of

218

injury or the decay of age, to helpless starvation. American citizenship should carry insurance against ruin through enforced idleness.

Our imagined leader might add, with universal approval: "America shall insure justice for all." Sadly short of that ideal do we fall today. No part of American government is more disgraceful—compared with the dictatorships—than the maladministration of law, and, more particularly, of criminal law. America needs a leader who will embody, as did Mussolini, in the idea of the State, the suppression, determined and ruthless, of organized crime, the final establishment of the supremacy of justice.

America also asserts the ideal of universal sound health. Every American citizen, having a prescriptive right to life, has logically a right to a sound body, a right to be well-born and well-bred. The right to be well-born involves the universal spread of the institutions for the care of mothers and babies that already flourish in many communities. A citizen of Alabama, because he is an American citizen, is entitled to as good community care in sickness as the new immigrant is given in New York City. The right to life and, therefore, to health, involves government insistence on the annihilation of hookworm and contagious diseases, the establishment and maintenance of sufficient hospitals throughout the land, and the provision of funds, through health insurance of various kinds, to insure that no American citizen shall be deprived of medical care whenever he needs it. Illness is one of the most prolific sources of want and misery. Americanism means that every citizen in times of peace shall be cared for in sickness as skilfully and certainly as the soldier is cared for in time of war. A sound body for every citizen—what a magnificent ideal! In that sound body each citizen shall be stimulated and empowered to cultivate a sound mind. No great nation is more fully committed to cultivating the sound mind than America. Salvation by education is the effective American creed. Despite the lapses from the observance of that article of faith, here and there, during the business depression, education for everybody, education varied to suit all capacities and talents, education limited only by the capacity to receive, is an inalienable part of Americanism. No dictatorship surpasses America in devotion to State education.

But the right to the best education becomes a mockery if not followed by the opportunity to work. A highly educated citizen may be a danger if the community does not so control its business machine as to furnish the willing student, on finishing his formal education, with a chance to use his powers for his own support and the service of the community. Recently an examination was held for the post of junior civil service examiner in Washington, at $1620 a year. Every applicant was required to hold a college degree. Of the 7,619 persons who took the examination 3,855 passed with gleaming honors. But there were only fifteen vacancies, though about eighty-five additional were appointed to other places which required a university degree. That was a demonstration of the plight of college youth today. They have been well trained by the State, given the best that the nation could discover for the development of mind and body, and then, through no fault of theirs, they can find no way to make a living. They form an educated and idle proletariat.

But America is girding its loins to struggle against that state of affairs. The leader we have been imagining would announce that Americanism shall include the opportunity of the educated youth to utilize his trained abilities in the needed work of the land.

If the industrial and commercial and financial organizations of the land were managed with the skill and foresight that would insure a job for every willing worker, the nation would be far on the road to the ultimate goal which our supposed inspired leader might announce as the destiny of America in the twentieth century—the Abolition of Poverty.

As the abolition of slavery and the overthrow of despotic power was the task of the nineteenth century, so the Abolition of Poverty is the task of the twentieth century. No nation is better equipped for that task than the United States, equipped with natural resources, industrial machinery and an intelligent and trained population.

Finally, the leader's definition of Americanism would take cognizance of youth's eagerness for altruistic service. America's youth has been at the receiving end of favors, rarely at the giving end. When war comes youth is asked for sacrifice unlimited; but, during peace, youth is not asked for any State service. The State gives him education without cost, often with a lavish generosity unequalled anywhere else. And youth is permitted to accept all the State's favors without thought of making any return. State service has been identified with soldier service. Our leader would dissipate that error. He would declare that America has need for return service by youth, a conscription for labor in place of the European conscription for warfare. America loses the few but important advantages which military conscription gives to other countries, advantages of training, discipline, intercourse among classes, the habit of obedience and ready cooperation. William James' moral substitute for war demands embodiment in institutions. It can't be got individually. Hitler has ordained that every German youth shall serve from six to twelve months in the labor camps—every youth, without discrimination in favor of wealth or education.

American democracy has not dared to impose on youth such an obligation. And youth remains indifferent to Americanism. The cure for Communism in the colleges is not the persecution of professors; but the formulation and preaching of real Americanism, the positive preaching of duty to the State, duty not in the trenches but in the home fields and factories, duty not to slay but to save, not to destroy but to create.

A year's service to the State by every youth, properly organized and led, might meet the demand for old-age sustenance of their collective parents. Formerly the children of the family sustained their father and mother in old age in the family homestead. Nowadays the children are usually scattered and the homestead has been abandoned for life in the city. The old folks are thrown on the State for support. But the State might, with advantage both to itself and to youth, provide that the children, before they started to serve themselves, should do their share jointly, all together, to meet the needs of the old. Youth pays little taxes; but youth is the time for cheerful work. So the State might call every boy to the colors, the industrial colors, to work together for the common good. He would get all the benefits that come from soldiering. He would discover by that experience that "Fellowship is life and the lack of fellowship is death." His patriotism would become positive. He would have a stake in the country. The shovel would supersede the sword. Each year Americans could make as brave a display as Hitler's Nazi camp workers did at Nuremberg when they went through their shovel evolutions with the precision and enjoyment of veterans. Surely an American labor camp could be made as educational, moralizing and valuable as the Red Soldier camps of Russia. An embryo exists in the Citizens' Conservation Camps, that part of the New Deal which has met least opposition and which is being doubled in size in 1935. Patriotism can be cultivated not by leaving youth free to follow its own desires with obligation to neither home nor State; but rather by establishing a positive ideal for America and boldly, continuously, enforcing that ideal. American youth would respond magnificently if summoned for service, not for war, but service to the works of God for sustenance, not to the works of the devil for death. Such service and obligation, which in the dictatorships is organized for the State in which "you, the individual, are nothing" can be organized under democracy for the welfare of the individual through the State; for the promotion of American ideals and American aims. With increased devotion we can modify the oath of allegiance which is taken in the schools, and recite:

"We swear allegiance to our flag and to the government for which it stands; one nation indivisible, with life, liberty, justice and *duty* for all."

INDEX

Abolition of Poverty, 220
Abyssinia, denied arbitration, 66
Advisory opinion, World Court, 8
Airplanes and parts not munitions of war, 80
Alexander I of Jugoslavia, assassination, 11, 13
America, an ideal for, 216; cure for Communism, 221; duty, 222; education, 220; health, 219; justice, 219; labor camps, 222; life, liberty and the pursuit of happiness, 218; opportunity to work, 220; patriotism, 217, 222; religion, 217; altruistic service by youth, 219; the leader, 217
American Bar Ass'n, World Court, 9
American democracy, and depression, 204; disadvantages, 202; future, 208, 209; fundamentals, 200.
American Federation of Labor, 200
American, interests in Far East, 56; legal system based on Magna Carta, 174; mercantile marine, 193; national unity, division, 207; neutrality, 36; opposition to League of Nations, 65, 67, 146; Peace Association, 5; scientific methods applied to public problems, 204; women's clubs, 71; youth, 216
Anglo-Saxons, 71
Anti-Trust Laws, failure in U. S., 205
Armaments investigation, U. S., 28; proponents in U. S., 185; limitations, U. S. treaty, 75
Aryans and Teutons, 141, 142
Assembly of the League of Nations, 8
Austria and the World Court, 8

Baker, Ray Stannard, introduction by, ix
Baldwin, Stanley, 32, 67, 146, 176
Ballila, Mussolini's child warriors, 124
Barthou, Louis, assassination of, 13
"Battle of Wheat", Italy, 72
Benes, Edouard, 14, 146
Biographical Sketch, xiii
Bissom, T. A., 79
Black Shirts, Italy, 115; Germany, 135; young, 215
Blum, Leon, 154, 161
Bolsheviks, 91
Booth, Charles, 179
Borah, Senator, 6
Bourgeoisie, defined by Marx, 95
Briand, M., 6
Brisbane, Arthur, 185
"Britannia rules the waves", 182
Brown Shirts, 132, 134
Bruening, Dr. Heinrich, 30
Bryan, William Jennings, 49

Butler, Harold, 15

CCC camps, U. S., 136, 222
Canada and the U. S., 71; "I'm Alone", 76
Chaco war, 10
Chamberlin, Sir Austin, 68
Chamberlin, Henry S., 96-100
Chamberlin, Houston Stewart, 141
Chiang Kai Shek, 55, 103
China, civil wars, 55, 71; grave of Japanese ambition, 74; open door policy, 53, 77; World Court, 9
Churchill, Winston, 176
Civil service, France, 160; Great Britain, 177; U. S., 203
Clay, Henry, U. S. internal improvement and tariff, 195
Clemenceau, Georges, 163
Codes of industry in the U. S., 205
Coolidge, Calvin, 30
Communism, 96; cure for, 221
COMMUNISM, RUSSIA AND, Chap. V, 89
"Communist Manifesto," 89
Communists, Young, 215
Company unions, 177, 178, 206
Corporations, development in the U. S., 196; government, in Italy, 122
Coty and the Solidarite Francaise, 156
Coughlin, Father, 65
Council, League of Nations, boycott against Germany, 35; condemnation of Germany, 17; Jugoslavia dispute determined by, 13, 14
Court of International Justice, 7
Covenant, League of Nations, 5, 9, 11, 35; history and effectiveness, 9; ineffective respecting Manchukuo, 11; non-intervention in revolutionary war, 70
Cripps, Sir Stafford, 179

Dantzig, 145
Das Kapital, "The Scriptures of Russia", 90
Daudet, Leon, (Action Francaise), 156
Davis, John W., 8
Davis, Norman H., 15, 16, 26, 54, 56
Dawes Plan, 164
Deladier, 158
Denmark and the World Court, 7
Democracies, overthrown, 173; three great, 147
Democracy, American, and the depression, 204; disadvantages, 202; future, 208; some fundamentals, 200; defined by Mussolini, 117; industrial revolution, 153; social, in America, 201

223

INDEX

DEMOCRACY IN THE U. S., Chap. X, 193

DEMOCRACY IN GREAT BRITAIN, Chap. IX, 173

DEMOCRACY OF FRANCE, Chap. VIII, 153

Depression, economic, in the U. S., 204; France, 155, 162; Germany, 73

Dictators bring war, 147

Dictatorships, established, 173; military tyrannies, 123

DICTATORSHIPS, YOUTH AND, Chap. VI, 215

DISARMAMENT, THE BREAKDOWN IN, Chap. II, 25

Disarmament Conference, 15; Germany withdraws, 30, 155

Dole, England, 181; France, 162

Dollfuss, Chancellor, assassination, 143

Doumergue, 160, 161

Dupont, Irenee, 28

Duranty, Walter, 97

Eden, Sir Anthony, 32, 67, 144, 146, 184

Embargo on arms to Chaco combatants, 10

Engels, Frederick, 89, 92

England, attitude toward League, 67; international democratic policies, 182; pioneer in civil liberties, 174; rejects laissez faire, 177, 180; "white paper", 67

Ernst, Herr, 132

Far East, U. S. policy, 79, 184

Farmers, France, 162; Germany, 135; Great Britain, 181; Italy, 72; Russia, 97; U. S., 204

Fascism, 111, 116-119, 122

Faulhaber, Cardinal, 140

Fischer, Louis, 97

Fisher, Sir John, 182

Five-Year Plan, 95, 101

Flandin, Pierre Etienne, 162

Ford, Henry,—mass production and mass consumption, 202

FRANCE, DEMOCRACY OF, Chap. VIII, 153

France, Albert Prince, murder, 161; appealed to League in 1935, 17, 66; civil service, 160; codes of industry, 163; disarmament conference, 27; economic distress, 153, 155; "Fascist coup d'etat", 157-160; foreign menace, 153, 155; Germany, 166; grievance against U. S., 163-165; House of Deputies, 154, 156, 159, 163; municipal pawn shops, 157; national security, 166; Neo-Socialists, 155; parliamentary instability, 153, 155; patriotic organizations, 156; radicals, 154; Stavisky scandal, 157; Socialists, 154; three quandaries, 153; unemployment, 162; war debts to U. S., 164; World Court, 7

Franck, Dr. Hugo, 140

French Indo-China, 56

French view of U. S., 163

Geneva Conference, 25; reason for breakdown, 30

George, Lloyd, 12, 27

German reparations, 165

GERMANY AND NATIONAL SOCIALISM, Chap. VII, 131

Germany, airfleet, 33, 144; Aryans and Teutons, 141, 142; standing army, 27, 33, 34, 134, 144; Austria, 143; Black Shirts, 135; "blood substance", 141; Communists, 133, 135; condemned by Council, 17; civil liberties sacrificed, 138; disarmament conference, 26; economic aims, 131, 135; failure of foreign trade, 36; farm property, 135; industry, 137; industrial depression, 73; internal strife, 132; Jews, 141; labor camps, 136; Labor Front, 138; monarchists, 135; navy, 144; Negroes, 141; Nordic myth, 140; probable demands by League, 69; purpose, 72; rearmament, 137, 144; Reichstag burned, 133; religious persecution, 139; revival of national spirit, 131, 132; Russia chief enemy, 70, 145; Saar plebiscite, 132; Treaty of Versailles, 69; unemployment, 136; welfare relief, 137; World Court, 8, 10; youth of, 215, 216

Goering, Herman Wilhelm, 132

Goebbels, Dr. Joseph, 132, 138

Gompers, Samuel, 15

Gorki, Mme. Maxim, 203

GREAT BRITAIN, DEMOCRACY IN, Chap. IX, 173

Great Britain, agriculture, 181; Carlyle, Ruskin and Kingsley, 177; dole system, 181; foreign trade, 179; government interest in League, 69, 145; Germany probable election issue, 146; home building subsidized, 181; India bill, 175; industrial system, 177, 178; joint security through League, 145; Labor Party, 178; naval conference, 37; poor relief funds, 181; public opinion supports League, 35; self-government, 175; South Africa, 183; the Dominions and the U. S., 184; social security, 179, 180; unemployment, 176; unemployment insurance, 181; World Court, 7; yellow journalism, 35; laws of neutrality, 81

Greek revolution, 71

Greenland and the World Court, 7

Green, William, 200

Hague, the, 7

Hardie, Keir, 178

Harding, Warren G., 183

Hay, John, 53

Hearst, William Randolph, 185; papers, 65

Herriot, M., 98, 154, 156, 159

Hindus and Mohammedans, 175, 176

Hindus, Maurice, 97

Hirota, Foreign Minister, 50, 55

Hitler, Adolf, 18, 31, 67, 73, 117, 131, 142; alienated Mussolini, 144; alienates American idealists, 167; alienates England, 167; declaration of defiance, 32, 144; declares for peace, 144; offers alliance against France, 144; State credo, 143; youth appeal, 215

Hoover, President, 26, 30, 164, 199, 208

Hughes, Charles Evans, 183

Hungary, return of nationals by Jugoslavia, 14

"I'm Alone" case, 76

Ideal State, the, of Dictators, 216

Industrial organization in Great Britain, 177, 178

Industry, codes of, in the U. S., 205; Germany, 73; organization of in Italy, 122, 205; stabilizing in the U. S., 202

Internal improvement and the tariff, U. S., Henry Clay, 195

International army in the Saar, 13

International Labor Office, 15

Introduction, by Ray Stannard Baker, ix

Inukai, Prime Minister, 48

ITALY AND FASCISM, Chap. VI, 111

Italy, Austria-Hungary, 31; Black Shirts, 115; Caporetti, 113; expansion, 124; Fighting Fascists, 115; government unions, 122; guild state threatened with extinction, 124; Mussolini becomes ruler, 116; national wealth, 72; organization of industry, 205; Poland, 144; Republican Party, 112; Socialist Party, 111; unemployment, 123

Jager, Dr., 139

JAPAN, MUST THE U. S. FIGHT? Chap. III, 47

Japan, attack upon China, 10, 35, 74; London naval conference, 37; nationalism, 47; nation meriting respect, 51; naval agreement, 183; newest comer among great powers, 57; program of empire development, 40, 72, 74; rasons for clashes with U. S., 53, 77; Russia and Germany, 79, 80; seeks export outlets, 53; World Court, 9; U. S. distrusts, 50, 58; U. S. exclusion act, 49; U. S. interference, 48; withdraws from World Court, 10

Japanese in the U. S., 53

Jefferson, Thomas, U. S. foreign policy, 81, 193

Johnson, General Hugh, 199, 206

Jugoslavia, return of Hungarian nationals, 14

Kamenof, 101

Kellogg Pact, 7, 11, 27; history and effectiveness, 9; ineffectual respecting Manchukuo, 11

KELLOGG PACT, LEAGUE OF NATIONS AND, IN PERSPECTIVE, Chap. II, 5

Knox, Geoffrey G., 12

Krupp, von, 137

La Rocque, Colonel de, fiery cross, 156

Laval, Pierre, 12, 164

LEAGUE OF NATIONS AND THE KELLOGG PACT IN PERSPECTIVE, Chap. II, 5

League of Nations, 5; American opposition, reasons, 65; boycott against Germany, 95; can prevent accidental war, 68; cannot prevent aggression, 68; cooperation of U. S., 15, 37; disarmament conference, 15; force impractical, 18; France, 166; Germany resigns, 30; Japan-China war, 10; most conspicuous failure of, 17; nonintervention in revolutionary war, 70; opposition factor in U. S., 185; peace with security? 66; lacks vigor, 66; prevent international war, 71; recognized agency of international cooperation, 17; successful without U. S., 16

League to Enforce Peace, 5

Lebrun, President, 160

Lenin, Nikolai, 89, 92

Lincoln, President, 196

Lippman, Walter, 57

Little Entente, 73

Litvinov, Maxim, 26

Locarno, Eastern, 34, 70

Lodge, Senator Cabot, 164

London, center of international finance, 173

London disarmament conference, 26, 37, 47

Londonderry, Lord and Lady, 178

Lothian, Lord, 78

Lowell, Dr. A. Lawrence, 57

Lyautey, Marshal, 160

MacDonald, James Ramsay, 26, 32, 164, 178

Magna Carta, 174

Mahatma Gandhi, 175

Manchukuo, non-resognition of, 11

Manchuria, 17, 47, 49, 74, 54, 57

Marx, Karl, 89, 92; fundamental doctrines, 92

Mass production and mass export, Germany, 73;

Mass production and mass consumption, U. S., 202

Mercantile marine, American, 193

Mitsubishi, House of, 47

Mitsui, House of, 47

Money and credit system in the U. S., 206

Morgan, J. P., 198

Morrison, Herbert, 180

Mueller, Reichsbishop Ludwig, 139

Munitions, airplanes and parts not considered, 80

Mussolini, Benito, 72, 111, 115, 124; a new cabinet, 122; cleaned up Italy, 120; Corporative State, 122; Fascist State, 119; road to ruin, 123; troops to Abyssinia, 66; youth appeal, 215

Napoleon, Mussolini following, 123

National unity, American, divisions appearing in, 207

INDEX

NATIONAL SOCIALISM, GERMANY AND, Chap. VII, 131
Naval ratios, 38
Naval treaties, U. S., Gr. Britain and Japan, 183; future of, 185, 186; results, 39, 47
Nazi Party, 133, 139
Nazism in Austria, 143
Neutral rights on sea, 77, 79, 80, 81
New Deal, the, 15
Noguchi, Japanese martyr to science, 5
Non-recognition of territory taken in contravention of covenants, 11, 49
Nordic myth, Germany, 140
Norway and the World Court, 7

OGPU, agent of Russian tyranny, 101
Open Door Policy, 53, 79
Outlawry of war, the, 6

Pacifist, defined, 102
Pact of Paris, 27
Pan American Conference, the, 10
Parliament of man, the League is a, 17
PEACE, WANTED: A NEW STRATEGY OF, Chap. IV, 65
Peace, neutral rights precedent to, 81; U. S., two doctrines, 77; with security
"Peace time patriotism", in America, 216
under League of Nations, debate, 66
Philippine Islands, 56, 79
Poincare, Raymond, 165
Poland, 145
Polish Corridor, 144
Poverty, Abolition of, 220
Proletariat, defined by Marx, 95
Prince, M. Albert, murdered, 161
Public problems, American scientific methods, 204

Queen Bess, 181
Quelch, Harry, 9

Radziwill, Princess Catherine von, 133, 135
Rand, Professor Gordon, 141
Rasputin, 93
Reading, Lord, 174, 176
Reemployment in the U. S., 206
Reichswehr, 27, 37, 133
Relief work, public, in the U. S., 206
Reparations, German, 165
Roehm, Ernst, 132, 133
Rogers, Will, 202
Rollins College under the Soviets, 101
Roman Empire, 72
Roosevelt, President, 16, 26, 29, 30
Roosevelt, Theodore, 48, 52
Root, Elihu, 7, 9
Russell, Bertrand, 94
RUSSIA AND COMMUNISM, Chap. V, 89
Russia, censorship, 98; collective farms, 97; Communism, 96; culture, 93; Das Kapital, "The Scriptures", 90; doctrine of class war, 92, 96; doctrine of surplus value, 92, 94; economic interpretation of history, 92; education, 100; famine, 97; Germany and Japan, 70, 80; industrialization of, 95; international policies, 102; League of Nations, 14; Marxian doctrines, 92; morals, 93; OGPU, 101; Red army, 103; religion, 93; seeks British aid vs. Germany, 145; Standard Oil Co., 104; State errors corrected, 95; trade union of writers, 94; U. S. policy, 104; unemployment, 96; Young Communists, 215

Saar, the, 11, 132
"Salvation by education", the American creed, 220
Scientific methods, American, applied to the control of public problems, 204
Scotland Yard, body guard sent to the Saar, 12
Security in America, an ideal, 216, et seq.
Shaw, George Bernard, 90
Siberia, invasion of, 49, 58
Simon, Sir John, 11, 32, 67, 69, 144
Simonds, Frank H., 70, 71
Slavery, abandonment, U. S., 92, 196
Smuts, General Jan Christian, 77, 78, 183, 184
Social Democracy in America, 201
Socialist Party in France, 154; in Italy, 111
Socialism, 91, 131
South Africa, 183
South America, 173
Spoils system, the, in the U. S., 203
Stalin, Josef, 89, 95, 101, 145, 216
Stanley, Lord, 182
State, American ideal of security in, 216, et seq.
Stavisky scandal, 157, 161
Stimson, Henry S., 11, 57
Stresa Conference, 33, 145
Streseman, Chancellor, 35
Sun Yat Sen, 74, 103

Tariff, internal improvement and U. S., Henry Clay, 195
Terboven, Herr, 140
Teutons and Aryans, 141, 142
Thomas, M., 15
Threadneedle Street, 173, 178
Togo, Admiral, 38
Tolstoi's Christian version of Socialism, 91
Treaty of Versailles, 27

Ukraine, 145
Unemployment, France, 162; Great Britain, 176; insurance, Great Britain, 118
Unions, company, 206; government, 122
UNITED STATES, MUST FIGHT JAPAN? Chap. III, 47
United States, abolition of slavery, 92, 196; British Dominions, 184; armaments commission, 75; armaments investigation, 28; Canada, 71; codes of industry, 205; cooperation with League of Nations, 15, 75, 76; development of corporations, 196; disarmament

226

INDEX

conference, 15, 29; distrust of Japan, 50, 58; economic depression, 204; failure of anti-trust laws, 205; forego neutral rights, 27; foreign policy, 76, 79, 80, 184, 193; France since the war, 163; George Washington and foreign policy, 18, 193; Geneva Conference, 26; "Im Alone", 76; internal improvement and the tariff—Henry Clay, 195; international labor conference, 15; isolation no longer endures, 16; Japan's stumbling block, 48; Japanese excluded, 49; Lincoln, tariff and homestead act, 196; mass production and mass consumption—Henry Ford, 202; money and credit system, 206; naval conference, 37; neutral rights on sea, 77, 79, 80, 81; non-recognition of non-treaty territory, 11, 49; organization of industry, 205; policies in Far East, 50, 74; powerful agency for peace, 16; public relief work, 206; reasons for clashes with Japan, 53; reemployment, 206; resuscitation of farmers, 204; Russian policy, 104; Senate defeats motion to join World Court, 65, 75; spoils system, 203; stabilizing industry, 202; Thomas Jefferson and foreign policy, 193; trade with China, 78; trade with nations at war, 36; two doctrines of peace, 77; war with Japan indicated, 78, 80; will avert war with Japan, 50; World Court, 7, 75

Versailles, Treaty of, 27, 31, 69, 164
Von Schleicher, General, 30, 132, 133, 134

Wagner, Frau, 134
War, accidental, aggrandizement, revenge, 68; foreign markets, 73; people of Europe opposed to, 146
Warren, Charles, 79, 80
Washington, George, and U. S. foreign policy, 18, 193
Weygand, General, 34
Webb, Beatrice and Sidney, 177, 179
Wells, H. G., 206
Winter Park under the Soviets, 100
Wilson, Woodrow, 5, 12, 18, 49, 163
World Court, 7, 17; advisory opinions of, 8; American adherence to, 9, 65; Japan withdraws, 10; U. S. Senate defeats motion to join, 65

Young Communists, 215
Young Plan, 164
YOUTH AND DICTATORSHIPS, Chap. XI, 215
Youth, an ideal leader for in America, 216, et seq.

Zinoviev, 101

227